By the same author

Out of the Ark

OVER THE STEPPING STONE

Rosalind Allan

HODDER AND STOUGHTON
LONDON SYDNEY AUCKLAND TORONTO

To Juliet, Rupert and Bridget

Scriptural quotations are from the Revised Standard Version of the Bible, unless otherwise indicated.

British Library Cataloguing in Publication Data
Allan, Rosalind
  Over the stepping stone.
  1. Christian life
  I. Title
  248.4

ISBN 0-340-51746 8

Copyright © Rosalind Allan 1990. First published in Great Britain 1990. All rights reserved. No part of this publication may be reproduced or transmitted in any form or by any means, electronic or mechanical, including photocopying, recording, or any information storage or retrieval system, without either prior permission in writing from the publisher or a licence permitting restricted copying. In the United Kingdom such licences are issued by the Copyright Licensing Agency, 33–34 Alfred Place, London WC1E 7DP. The right of Rosalind Allan to be identified as the author of this work has been asserted by her in accordance with the Copyright, Designs and Patents Act 1988.

Published by Hodder and Stoughton, a division of Hodder and Stoughton Ltd, Mill Road, Dunton Green, Sevenoaks, Kent TN13 2YA. Editorial Office: 47 Bedford Square, London WC1B 3DP.

Photoset by Avocet Robinson, Buckingham

Printed in Great Britain by Cox & Wyman Ltd, Reading.

CONTENTS

	Introduction	vii
1	Over the Stepping Stone	1
2	Saying Grace – or Possessing It?	5
3	Suffer Me to Come to Thee	19
4	In a Mysterious Communion	33
5	Jesus' Supper Party	41
6	"I See'd God!"	49
7	For Making Me Me!	59
8	Airing that Tea-Bag	71
9	A Bus-Load of Boffins	83
10	"All Gone, a Devil!"	103
	References	114

INTRODUCTION

I am not a great dreamer in the ordinary sense of the word. But I have had particular dreams that transformed my reactions and caused me to allow my career to be re-routed. These dreams were unsought; they did not relate to recent subconscious notions about everyday experiences; they were new, fascinating, sometimes very challenging and could always be aligned with what I had understood of the Bible.

In *Out of the Ark* I told how it was through a God-given dream that I was able to understand the joy and fun now being experienced by Penelope, our daughter who died, and how concerned she is for Hugh and me, her parents. It was through another dream that God enabled me and others to start the Ark Christian Book Centre and Coffee Shop, where other people of all denominations could receive the strength and encouragement I had received from Christ's risen Body. Out of that came the dream for the first ever Good News van. That was a real challenge, because, as I have told in *Out of the Ark*, it met with plenty of opposition, and not only from the money-minded secular world. Christians thought there must be a catch, that money (or, yes indeed, your time!) would be required by someone, despite the fact that we ran a completely free lending library, with no strings attached. Bookshops gradually recognised the tremendous value of unofficial "reps" in the form of van teams who constantly recommend current publications, and who allow borrowers to have a preliminary read at home. Then the Good News Trust was formed, when a local clergyman called Martin Down left his parish work temporarily and came with his family to live and work with us for four years. Martin and I studied the story of the Feeding of the Five Thousand and knew that we must, like the disciples, sit people down in "companies" (house-groups) and feed them ourselves. Hence the numerous practical Bible Study "Do-Its" (John 2:5) which are now being sent free of charge wherever requested all over Britain. Out of that has sprung the nationwide network of caring, renewed Christians so important to those still feeling solitary in their search for the living Lord.

It was then, too, that our own family, Hugh and I, Juliet, Rupert and Bridget, had to reconsider how best to fulfil Jesus' command not only to love the Lord our God "with all our hearts", but also our new, resident neighbours, as ourselves! Experience of living as a two-family household or "community" has taught us plenty about other people's preferences in Christian work and worship. Experience of the contributions other denominations can make to our thinking and behaviour has come with new friendships made in the Good News van work. The calamities, dismay, encouragement and discovery of all this constitute this book.

The scars and wounds in the Body of Christ, His Church, are so many that newcomers are sometimes distressed, ready to part company with the established, so often warring, denominations. How the Devil must exult! But our Lord is triumphant. By a curious device, provided we are willing, our Heavenly Father makes something yet more splendid from the Devil's debris. The stepping stone mentioned in the dream in the first chapter of this book seemed at first dirty and ugly. It is only at God's touch that tiny fish scurry around so joyously. It is only as we begin to perceive the beauty of each denominational facet of the whole stepping stone under the burnishing and refining of the Holy Spirit, that it can gradually be looked upon as a diamond. The beauty of a diamond lies in its many facets, as they reflect and break up the light; the glory of God's Church lies in

Introduction

the way each denominational facet, once it is seen as part of the whole, similarly and gradually will reflect the Light of the World. With the most perspicacious comments of all coming, quite innocently, from my children, I have learned to trust the possibility of the diamond becoming apparent.

Over the Stepping Stone could not have been written without the early help and encouragement of Martin Down who helped me to set to work and reduce it to simple proportions, and my husband Hugh who insisted that I word matters clearly! Jenny Gosling took an intelligent and encouraging interest in the manuscript as she typed most of it. It was Juliet Newport, my editor at Hodder, who sensitively sorted out the final proofs.

Above all I have to thank our children, whose comments and behaviour captured the spirit of what I wanted to say, and who were not too abashed to go on record.

Rosalind Allan

1

OVER THE STEPPING STONE

It all began at a Quiet Day at Edward King House, high on a hill adjacent to Lincoln Cathedral. Each of us had been sent off to listen, on our own, to the Lord. I was unsure that I would be able to relax for long in the state of attentive, creative silence that allowed complete freedom for the Lord to speak. My companions looked formidably isolationist, competently still, quite unaware of anyone else. I decided to settle in a window seat which commanded a view first into the garden, then down into the seething city and thence far out into the misty greens of the open countryside. If I was to hear the Lord at all, it might be through contemplating those scenes; if not I could draw pictures and just think.

Then I realised I did not have to be skilled in a particular form of meditation. I could try Jesus' own instruction for a start: "When you pray, say 'Our Father'."

I tried the first phrase, very slowly. Immediately I felt as if I was a little girl aged about three. The scene had changed completely. In my thinking, I was playing on dry mud by a broad river. I was on the low bay of land created by cattle over the years when they plodded down to drink at the stream. On a grassy tussock to my right sat my Heavenly Dad. Excited and expectant, I tried to understand how I could play. The earth was trodden flat and barren. The surrounding grass held no interesting or beautiful flowers. I had no toys with me. I turned enquiringly to my Heavenly Father.

"Find a beautiful stone. Go on. You know you like to bring one home from every outing, so as to remember it."

I thought of the pretty stones I had often come across on a pebble beach: when wet they were beautiful. I stared at the dirty river; its bed was strewn with a few weed-draped, squared stones, perhaps debris from building work. There was nothing attractive or small enough for me to pick up. Impatiently my Heavenly Dad reached into the middle of the river and shifted one of the larger, shiny stones. Instantaneously a scurry of tiny silver fish danced into sight. I was delighted; but as soon as He withdrew His hand the river mud settled again and the fish slid out of sight.

I stared, puzzled, wondering what should happen now. Then very gradually the stone grew and grew until I realised it had broken through the surface of the water. It was a brilliantly sunny day so the top of the stone dried out quickly. At last I realised what it was and what I could do.

"It's a stepping stone!" I exclaimed. "I love stepping stones. Can I go over to the other side?" The far bank looked gloomy and a little forbidding, but I longed to explore the woodland over there. At least it was lush, compared with the arid bank where I stood.

"Yes. You may go over there. But I don't want you to stay there. You are to come back, bringing the people who are there with you. Make sure that they come loaded with the treasures of their ancient wisdom and culture."

I imagined people trudging out of the forests I could glimpse, laden with great gold-edged icons, gold and silver goblets, marble sculptures . . .

"What is that stepping stone?" I asked.

"That shall be the subject of your next book."

I thought about that scene for more than a year before I could seriously tackle it. Then one or two matters became clear to me.

First the Lord had shown me myself as a little child, not

Over the Stepping Stone

a babe in arms but a fairly sturdy, active small person, impatient for things to happen. In terms of the Kingdom, that is what I am. Although I was reared a churchgoer from birth, it is only in recent years that I have come to know the beginnings of fullness of life in the Holy Spirit. I was standing around wondering what to do, in order to relish the abundance of that life.

I was standing on an arid bank, sunny with the joy of the Lord's presence, but devoid of anything with which to enjoy Him. Since my baptism in the Holy Spirit I have experienced with joy and wonder the glory of His presence. I have attempted to express that delight in all the ways practised by my elders and betters in the Spirit-filled life: singing happy choruses over and over again, raising my arms heavenwards, clapping, dancing, playing the tambourine, flute or piano; by responding to the warmth of loving hugs; by singing or speaking in tongues and by moving in the gifts of the Spirit as far as I dared; by attending rallies and conferences. All the time I have been aware of the facets of the Christian life that few of my Spirit-filled friends care about any longer and I feel dry and wistful, standing as it were on a sunny but dried-out and gritty bank, gazing at the big, brown river.

As I wondered what I could do, my Heavenly Father had suggested that I collect a stone, an attractive one, by which to identify and remember this outing. I had seen nothing suitable, either on the bank or glinting at me through the water. In the charismatic world I had the hang of what to do in worship, but that was becoming mechanical, almost dry from custom. The worship I had previously been involved in was dry from custom already, a tradition of men rather than Spirit-inspired, deep devotion. What could I find through which to share real friendship and delight with the Lord and with His children? What I could see on the bed of the river was uniform and uninteresting. It took the touch of my Heavenly Father to disturb things and arouse a scurry of new life.

The countryside on the far bank of the river had looked heavily wooded, a little dense and gloomy in the distance. But, in contrast to the barrenness of the earth where I stood, the farther bank was lush with long grass by the river; over there the sky was overcast, but flowers and shrubs were abundant; there was plenty for a child to explore. If I was to understand that to be the land of the established denominations, then it looked exciting and interesting.

I knew I had to go via that stepping stone with the attitude of a little child, and I had to come back with what I had learned.

2

SAYING GRACE – OR POSSESSING IT?

It was one of those days when, if I were to stop for breath, I would have screamed, "Let's just stop and start all over again! Back to where we were, please!" And I would have waited for time to roll back to a point in life before I was renewed in the Spirit, when I could keep up with what was happening, sit back and assess the situation, make plans for a predictable, if very dull, future.

As it was, the ordinary pattern of life had suddenly been interrupted. We had been a family of five living in an eight-bedroomed, three-bathroomed house. The top floor had been converted into a flat and let to help pay the mortgage.

The number of Good News vans had started to grow, and there were now eight little library vans lending lively Christian paperbacks wherever invited.

We had begun, three years earlier, with the first Good News Mini-van. My friend Margaret and I had taken, free of charge, Christian paperback library books and, later, tapes, wherever anyone invited us. Soon we were run off our feet. Another team volunteered to go out in a second van, and so it had gone on until there were eight vans and I was a member of four weekly interdenominational house-groups. Then Martin Down, vicar of a village more than ten miles away, joined the work. As far as we could understand the Lord's purposes, he and I were to rationalise the task of organisation, encourage several more van teams across the nation, visit, care for and pray for them all, and produce Bible Study material and encouragement in other ways for house-groups across Britain. Meanwhile his wife, Maureen, had opted to man the local van and expand its activities. She was also a trained secretary. We found we all needed to co-operate closely with one another, liaising over both practical and theological issues. Moreover, since this was an interdenominational charity, we needs must share our lives together if this work was to thrive. The house we lived in was big enough to house two families. If the Lord was calling us to this work, we would need to depend entirely on Him for our material needs. This was particularly true for Martin and his family. He felt called to commit himself to share in this work, but because it was interdenominational there was no way in which he felt justified in continuing to be paid and housed by the Church of England. Our house was big enough to share with him, his wife Maureen and their two children, provided we re-established the flat as our own living accommodation and disposed of half a house of furniture to make way for theirs. The mortgage would now be entirely in the hands of the Lord as He guided my husband Hugh, who was a schoolmaster.

Today was removal day. The front door of our tall Victorian semi swung open and slammed shut every time the back door was opened, yet again for furniture to be adjusted and heaved upstairs, or outside to be stored in our garage. Half our furniture and half that of the Down family had gone to the sale-room. Now the empty rooms — a sitting-room on the ground floor and three bedrooms upstairs — were rapidly filling with vicarage furniture. Ben, our labrador-boxer dog, made off surreptitiously out of the back garden to explore the neighbours' dustbins; some of the rooms smelt of freshly dried paint; the kettle on the Aga was boiling itself dry — and the telephone was ringing yet again.

"This is the sale-room, Mrs Allan. What am I supposed to do with all this rubbish you have sent me?"

Saying Grace – or Possessing It?

My mind raced. We had sent him our best double bed, the one reserved for special guests. We had sent elderly armchairs, a settee and a table or two.

"I'm sorry the chairs are a little shabby," I admitted, "but the bed is a good one."

"Good? Did you say good? Can't sell beds to anyone these days. Tip's the best place for all this, if you ask me. But we're closing in ten minutes. Do you want it all taken to the tip, or shall we dump it back on your front lawn? My men are waiting for your instructions."

My mind skimmed over the furniture we had sent to the sale-room. It was the sort of thing we had been reluctant to part with; but that was probably more for sentimental reasons than for any inherent beauty or grace. Wherever would we put it, if it did come back? The furniture belonging to Martin and Maureeen Down was already in place. They had disposed similarly of some of their possessions in order to come and join us in the work of the Good News Trust. Was I going to cling on to much-loved but well-worn beds and armchairs, merely for old times' sake? They were only things, I told myself.

"Oh, send it all to the tip, please," I decided.

Then I went to rescue the kettle. A mug of good, strong tea was necessary for us all now. After all the Downs had announced their intention to eat and drink with us. Since we were attempting to live together as a household, obviously we should have meals together – and consoling drinks.

Both then and during the next few months events took place at great speed. I needed to remind myself why we were all throwing out so much of our privacy and self-sufficiency, and so many of our possessions. There should be some fundamental purpose for our coming together to live in community. But this was going to prove easier said than done. It was easy enough to understand and feel the rightness of what we were doing, but from the outset, and for the next year or two, we had to learn the difference between "it feels right" and "it feels comfortable and familiar".

In the early stages I felt uncomfortable, strange and yet excited to see what the Lord would do. Just how much I was listening to the details of His day by day instructions was another matter. We had all experienced the renewal of our lives through the Holy Spirit; but when it came to modes of living and praying, and to relationships within God's heavenly family, we were infants. The world was fresh and joyous: but as two families come together to share in God's work, how should we relate our old, secular ways to the new paths? It was essential, once the flurry of removal was over, to think through what the Lord intends for people He has called to live in community. Even the word "community" seemed pretentious, considering the humdrum people we were.

We were clear about one thing: we were aware that Martin, ordained in the Church of England, was accustomed to say morning and evening prayer. It was sound sense to join him, as a basis of worshipping together. So every weekday at twenty to eight, bleary-eyed or yawning, we assembled in the sitting-room to say the prayers, canticles and psalms for morning worship and listen to one or other of us reading the Bible passages prescribed by the Anglican Lectionary. At nine thirty in the evening we reassembled and followed the Alternative Service Book's evening prayer. We always ended the formal service with informal praises and prayer requests, which revealed something of our delights, anxieties and hopes as people trying to apply God's word to our attempts to live together. One day the prescribed passage was from Acts 2:44–46 GN:

> All the believers continued together in close fellowship and shared their belongings with one another. They would sell their property and possessions, and distribute the

Saying Grace – or Possessing It?

money among all, according to what each one needed. Day after day they met as a group in the Temple, and they had their meals together in their homes, eating with glad and humble hearts . . .

It was easy to draw some parallels. We had had to "sell our possessions and goods", primarily to make room for one another. In fact I had allowed some of our goods to go to the town tip, mainly through incompetence and harassment at the wrong moment! The proceeds from the sale of the rest of our surpluses had gone towards financing the new household and the needs of the Good News ministry. "Breaking bread in their homes, they partook of food with glad and generous hearts" (Acts 2:46). If we were to interpret "breaking bread" as partaking in Communion, then that would eventually have to be considered carefully, bearing in mind our denominational origins. But for the first few months we were concerned as much with sharing possessions and food.

Before we came together as a household we had experimented a little. The two families had gone on holiday, staying in a cottage on a headland on the southernmost tip of Holy Island beyond Anglesey, which we knew well. We had bought a pineapple as a treat; however, once Martin had cut it open we adults realised that its ripeness had degenerated to a soggy brownness. Nevertheless the fruit still tasted good so we smothered it in custard. It was that evening that the youngsters had planned to celebrate the end of the holiday with a barbecue half-way down a rock-strewn cliff, and so we bundled the "pineapple custard" into a gallon-sized ice-cream carton and set out. The weather was perfect. The driftwood fire already lit by the boys drew well. The aroma of frying sausages, beefburgers and onions rose on the wood smoke. We climbed down the rocks, guitar and ice-cream carton balanced, and relished the evening sunset. The young people produced an excellent meal and we were reluctant to bring the party to an end, especially as Juliet, our elder daughter, was strumming on the guitar, having heard that music attracts seals towards humans.

As we sang quietly in harmony, hoping we might glimpse the inquisitive pate of a seal, a yacht with great red sails crept silently round the cliff-head. We had eaten well, despite the curious lumps in the pineapple custard; our fellowship was good, laced with warm jokes and goodwill. "Ship ahoy!" we called to the red-sailed vessel. With confidence we too planned to launch out into uncharted waters.

But over the ensuing months our gratitude and goodwill were tested. Loving friends, discovering that we were a household of nine, in effect a community brought together by God to be used by Him, brought us gifts, as God's people have done from the time of the prophets to the days of the early church, and from the monastic era, to the present day. Our big trouble was that we had not considered how to receive them, especially in the present setting, no longer that of a sun-bathed evening barbecue but of a boisterous, demanding household of ravenous teenagers and their friends. None of us was accustomed to receiving large donations of food. Our English reserve prompted us to protest, "Oh, no. You really shouldn't. Don't you need this yourselves?" It was even more difficult when the gift was not normally a family favourite. English monastic foundations, if not the early church, would have accepted an abundance of rhubarb and gooseberries with glad and thankful hearts. Our youngsters had lost the knack – and so had we. Blessedly our fat copy of Mrs Beeton provided us with plenty of camouflage recipes.

Other guests arrived, bearing carrier bags: "These apples do need to be eaten soon, because they are a little bruised . . . they're fallens . . . they have little visitors." Rows of apple jelly swiftly appeared in the store-cupboard. This, I see now, was done with a good sense of stewardship worthy of any monastic order. The disgraceful aspect was that I had

Saying Grace — or Possessing It?

labelled the jars "Fallen Glory" or "Little Visitors' Delight". In fact gratitude and goodwill did abound, and we enjoyed all sorts of treats provided by loving friends who came, near the beginning, to share our house-warming.

But we did need to learn, ourselves, how to share. Beyond the evidence in the Bible, what sort of precedent was there in the immediate Christian world? I hunted through my books. The places where Christian community life had lasted were the monastic orders. A fat lot I knew about them, I thought dismissively. Then I found in the bottom of a drawer full of mementoes a duplicated "Interim Rule of the Sisters of Notre Dame" in Washington, DC. I had been given this for assessment and comment, by a nun I had met when we lived in the United States. It had been of no personal interest to me then, because I had not even attempted to imagine how, as a family, we could live in community. Now I leafed through its pages: "Only by the gift of ourselves to others can we build a community of love." "Unless the grain of wheat dies, itself remains alone." How could I apply that? How were we to give ourselves, now, to the others in our household?

I went on rummaging through the drawer until I came across a ginger-brown booklet. Several years before my renewal in the Holy Spirit I had discovered the Third, or Tertiary, Order of St Francis. This is a network of Anglican Christians committed to the three monastic vows: poverty, chastity and humility. Since the Third Order consists neither of monks nor nuns, but of people who are in the world, and often married, their commitment is modified appropriately. They still live in tune with the vows. In my search, which was eventually satisfied in the baptism of the Holy Spirit, I had become a learner-Tertiary, a postulant of the Third Order of St Francis, and had acquired this booklet. There was a section on poverty. The general exhortation was towards frugality:

> The Brothers and Sisters of the First and Second Orders
> LIVE AS FAMILIES, SHARING EVERYTHING . . .
> The members of the Third Order . . . should also aim at
> being free from all attachment to wealth and material
> gain, keeping themselves aware of the poverty of the world
> and of its claim upon their stewardship. So we shall reflect
> in spirit our Lord's counsel to sell all, give to the poor
> and follow Him.

When I was first baptised in the Holy Spirit I had abandoned the Third Order, on the grounds that it was too denominational in its general approach; now I began to see the appropriateness of the manual to our daily living. We had been willing enough to "sell all" in order to give to the spiritually hungry through Christian books. But we were somewhat fastidiously accumulating this world's goods, not being used as clear channels for dispensing whatever came our way.

The Third Order manual is plain about possessions: "The Brothers and Sisters of the First and Second Orders . . . accept no salary for themselves and own no personal possessions." "Members of the Third Order are to steward their essential property." We had, with charismatic zeal, agreed to live in the same house, but our possessions remained very much our own, except when it came to cars. We had acquired no fewer than five vehicles; one was the local Good News van; the second a Mini given to me specifically for my ministry; the third an elegant Allegro owned by the Down family but too small to transport the whole household; the fourth was the Allan family rusty old Mirafiori estate; and the fifth a small Simca saloon with a very low mileage, hardly driven but much cherished by an elderly uncle who had since died. We needed the Good News van, the Mini and a roomy household car.

"What are we to do with this lot, Lord?" I prayed.

Soon after the Downs joined us my husband Hugh sold

Saying Grace – or Possessing It?

the Mirafiori on the ordinary market. However it became clearer and clearer that that was not to be the way for the other cars. Although the rusty old Mirafiori was sold for £119, no one wanted the impeccably maintained Allegro and Simca; but neither of these would carry more than a small family. One day Martin remarked that he had seen just the vehicle for us all in a local garage. It was a Peugeot 504, costing £2,000. We had no income from the sale of the Allegro and Simca with which to barter but I still had £2,100 in savings — one of my little securities in this whirlpool of living in community. Temptation and the Lord vied with one another in my cogitations. I was reminded of private dreams of a holiday some day, abroad maybe, just Hugh and me . . . Then I thought of Ananias and Sapphira in the book of Acts, who secretly held back some of what they professed to be sharing. Eventually I admitted I had the money, and silently stamping and screaming with reluctance offered to pay. It was as the great navy-blue Peugeot 504 received from Martin its benediction of a "Thank God for Jesus" sticker that I knew that this was right. But we still had those other two cars.

Then the Lord put a new understanding into my mind: "Remember the rhubarb and the gooseberries. Freely you received. Freely you SHOULD have given those, long ago. Surely you have enough!"

"But we can't give away beautiful cars like those, Lord. People don't. We'll look peculiar trying to do that. We can't!" I protested. Those thoughts of a holiday abroad again sauntered into my mind.

There was no further comment.

"Have you any suggestions about these cars?" asked Martin. "We can't sensibly go on taxing and insuring the lot."

I felt very stupid as I mumbled, "Why don't we just give them away?" and I added as more responsible-sounding, "After all, we have tried to sell them. Perhaps we were asking too much; but if we asked less, people would wonder why. So I think we ought to give them away."

Inside I was wondering how I proposed replenishing my savings account so as to maintain the car I used for my work. However, if we were supposed to share our goods and possessions with the needy, we had better get on with it among those who had expressed a need.

There were several of these, one or two of whom had previously asked to borrow the Good News van for private purposes unconnected with a Christian book service. We had pointed out that the van had been given to us for a specific purpose and it was not ours to lend. Now, however, we did have two immaculately maintained vehicles available.

We telephoned an elderly couple who were much involved in ferrying their friends to the shops or to Christian gatherings. I knew their own car was costing them too much in repairs. But their answer came: "We'd prefer to hang on to what we have. At least we know its weaknesses."

I called on a father of a large family. He had several weekend preaching engagements in nearby villages and only a small part-time job.

"Would you like a well-maintained Allegro estate car, free?" I offered.

He looked at me narrowly, remarked that that was very kind, but that he would have to think about it.

A couple who worked in a local shop had often remarked how useful it would be if they had a company car. They had not been offered one. "Well, here is a choice of two, completely free," I ventured, knowing that my incredulous voice implied that they were at least bad lots, if not stolen!

The response from both the couple and the family man: "We could not afford the tax and insurance. Sorry."

Angry and frustrated that Christian people were treating our cars as we ourselves had responded to rhubarb and gooseberries, I telephoned London, where Auntie Penny,

Saying Grace – or Possessing It? 15

recently healed and converted, lived a purposeful Pentecostal life.

"Do you know anyone who'd like a good car, free?" I explained why.

'Oh, yes, yes, yes!" she exclaimed. "Carol needs one desperately. She's not a believer; that might help her to understand what I'm on about. And our pastor and his wife need transport. How wonderful!"

Within days we received a visit from Auntie Penny, her pastor and his wife. The cars were lined up, polished and gleaming on the bank opposite our house. Without any embarrassment at the public setting, cars whizzing up and down a main road into town, and rows of windows behind which any number of neighbours could be lurking, Auntie Penny asked her pastor to hold a small service of blessing. "Oh well," I thought, shamefacedly, "the neighbours must already have decided that we're extremely odd." Then I concentrated on praising God, eyes firmly closed. At last those cars were in use, purring off to the big city.

When, months later, we too purred off, not to the great metropolis, but to Prestatyn for Spring Harvest, the big Peugeot felt very good, and that was partly because Auntie Penny had sent me a cheque for £2,000, "for my personal use"; perhaps in the establishment of our new household?

I thought again of the Third Order manual: "their reserves ought not to exceed the strictly necessary". Our reserve of vehicles had been colossal. Gradually I began to see how bumbling and superficial had been what I had accepted as the norm in renewed life in the Holy Spirit of Jesus. I had missed so much in rejecting what had seemed dead and legalistic in the established frameworks of the denominations. I had failed to catch sight of the flashes of wisdom that lay as a rich seam in so much of their history. Almost unawares we had accumulated, first fallen apples, then rhubarb and gooseberries, finally cars. And we had no grace to receive them gladly and re-channel them, until we began to learn the Kingdom way in that improbable disposal of cars. At last the teaching of St Francis was beginning to be applied in my life.

It was not merely in the deployment of personal property that we born-again charismatics were too easily bewildered. We had not yet learned how to be gracious and loving with one another. First I had wanted to "stop the world and get off" when my personal privacy was being disrupted; everyone else must have felt similar, if not worse, but we each either flailed around trying desperately to defer to each other's needs in an ongoing hosts and guests situation, or withdrew into the guaranteed privacy of a bedroom. What we would have done amidst the hardships, starvation, imprisonment and shipwreck that Paul and his companions endured, I do not know. Subconsciously I have probably assumed that he was of the rough-and-ready, outward-bound breed, not the well-heeled, well-cushioned Pharisee of refined, scholarly breeding that he had been. Yet Paul had the audacity to count all this suffering gain! We learned to put up with all our little inconveniences with glum determination.

We had set far too little store by the old denominations. In their wisdom both the Salvation Army and the Catholic Church have taught and lived Paul's injunction to "rejoice in the Lord always" and to "be careful for nothing". General Booth taught his soldiers not only to share their belongings but also often their lives among the poor, to the triumphant witness of the army band and songsters. The Catholic calendar commemorates saints and martyrs whose names mostly mean nothing to the general run of today's charismatics. The ancient narrative of his martyrdom records that Polycarp, who died about AD 155, had been betrayed and arrested one evening at a farm outside Smyrna. He was taken into the city and led before the proconsul in the stadium, where a crowd was assembled for the games. The proconsul urged him to forswear his religion.

"Take an oath by the emperor's guardian spirit; curse Christ."

"I have served Him for eighty-six years, and He has done me no wrong," answered Polycarp. "How can I blaspheme my king and saviour?"

Polycarp was ordered to be burnt alive. He uttered a PRAYER OF PRAISE AND GLORY TO GOD and when he had offered up himself and said Amen, the fire was kindled "and the flames made a sort of arch, like a ship's sail filled with wind, and they were like a wall round the martyr's body; and he looked, not like burning flesh, but like bread in the oven or like gold or silver being refined in a furnace".

That lovely charismatic old man gloriously allowed them to burn him to death for his faith.

"Like bread in the oven", we had to learn carefully from centuries past how to allow ourselves to be broken and shared, maybe at first in simple matters such as allowing others to enjoy the good things, spiritual, cultural or material, in our lives in the home God had so graciously given us all.

3

SUFFER ME TO COME TO THEE

Eleven years before our coming together as a household our two older children, even if they had not heard of Polycarp, had come to know some of the idiosyncrasies of being an Anglican. Juliet, aged almost five, had started at the local church-aided primary school and Rupert, then three, was longing for the fun she obviously enjoyed. One day we were given a new insight into what Juliet understood as worship — as it was practised by infants in primary school.

Bridget, the youngest, and still our daughter-to-be, had deferred her arrival into the world, and so my husband devised his own way of speeding matters up. One bleak November Saturday afternoon he loaded Juliet, nine weeks into infant school, Rupert, aged three and a half, and expectant me into our elderly plum-red Bedford Dormobile. We rattled and bounced our way through the fog, tipping and jerking until we reached the village church of Cold Overton. The village was appropriately named for such an expedition, but Hugh the secondary schoolmaster tried to enliven the afternoon by exhortations to his family to consider the corbels, gargoyles and vaulting. Hugh was also hoping that my insides had been sufficiently joggled for our new baby to explode into the world by November the Fifth. "Not so!" retorted my insides, and so I began to appreciate and draw Hugh's attention to the bright kneelers in the pews.

Juliet's high voice suddenly commanded our attention: "Hands together! Eyes closed!"

I looked up. She had clambered into the pulpit, closely followed by her admiring brother, who was behaving like a mountaineer churchwarden.

"I said, hands together." She glared ferociously at otherwise empty pews. "Eyes closed, Mummy!"

We submitted, wondering what was to follow. Rupert, half-way up the pulpit stairs, paused and stared in silence until, faced with the preacher's gaze, he scrumpled up his eyes in obedience.

"Thank you, Go-o-ond. A-bah-de-bee, a-bah-de-bah. A-bah-de-be, a-bah-de-bah. Ah-MEN!"

"Amen," Hugh and I echoed.

"Now we'll sing a song." She held the nearest pulpit book open authoritatively, but upside-down. "Find number ninety-nine: 'Baa baa black sheep'." There was a respectful pause. Then Juliet's little voice piped up, accompanied by a knowledgable growl from Rupert:

> Baa baa, black sheep,
> Have you any wool?

Woolly-headed they were about worship. Whatever went on in their heads to distinguish all this awesome nonsense from the intimate conversations with Jesus they had at bedtime prayer at home? From the day they were born our children were able to hear us telling their Heavenly Father how glad we were that each of them had been created and telling Him how sorry we were when we knew we had spoilt things. That had grown into much more personal conversation, eventually developing into an ongoing one-to-one relationship. I am not sure that Juliet ever made any connection between that and the formal worship she experienced in school. As I read now about stalwart Polycarp, I wonder whether he too had a public manner and a totally private way of talking with his Lord. That would comfort me, because I am not convinced that I have yet

Suffer Me to Come to Thee

bridged that gap! But then I first had to come to an awareness of the Person with whom I could eventually chat.

As a little girl I too was taught to "say my prayers" at bedtime. I remember feeling that I was working my way through some sort of a task. Before I was allowed to snuggle down I had to kneel by my bed at my mother's knee and recite:

> Gentle Jesus, meek and mild,
> Look upon a little child.
> Pity mice in plicity,
> Suffer me to come to thee.

I remember being vaguely anxious about the mice; but I had no intention of revealing my ignorance of their pitiable whereabouts to a brother who would tease me mercilessly, nor even to my parents who might somehow, as they so often did, find it amusing enough to tell other adults. A little later, repeating the Lord's Prayer fast ranked almost as important as being able to say the alphabet backwards. Either seemed to promote me in the estimation of my brother John, five years older and five years more exclusive in all forms of fun and adventure.

Then I observed one day that John did not speak aloud when he prayed; moreover I was not supposed to have seen him at it, because prayer was private and awesome. With this discovery came the instruction that I should say sorry to God for all the things I had done wrong each day. It was bad enough having to say sorry to my family. To have to remember all my faults at night and say sorry to this invisible, all-knowing God was very depressing. I had become well aware of the strength of all-powerful, angry adults who knew me and loved me. There was no telling whether God could really put up with me. I had been told again and again that God loved everyone well enough to send His Son to a cruel death on their behalf; but were there limits to His tolerance? About this time I learned the words "wrath" and "judgment". No wonder private prayer ought to be silent.

It is easy for a small child to take for granted that what adults say, at least one to another, and probably more necessarily in formal language to an almighty God, will be partly unintelligible, merely a matter for future learning. It took me years therefore to question the sense of the "Gentle Jesus" prayer. Presumably God, the all-knowing, would understand what was intended, and certainly reciting it freed me to scramble into bed. The whole business of what I had quite unwittingly done to His Son was well beyond me and very embarrassing. Jesus Himself was entirely devoid of personality; but the grown-ups seemed to love Him, in a dutiful, wishy-washy way. Perhaps when I grew up I would find out why.

The language of learned prayer did nothing to bring me a clearer understanding of the Person with whom I was supposed to be communicating. I had seen the words "gentle" and "mild" on Milk of Magnesia bottles. The cream inside the dark blue bottle was pure white and very good for sorting out my insides when I had been greedy.

It was the same with the Lord's Prayer. I estimated that that ought to be intelligible to most sensible people, considering Jesus was teaching His disciples the rudiments of prayer. Big people had made it clear that the Lord's Prayer was utterly simple. Privately I was ashamed that nearly every line used phraseology that was foreign to me. It was a relief, a few years later, to laugh with, rather than at, friends who shared my bewilderment at the Chart in Heaven and at having to call our Heavenly Father "Hallo". God was both remote and unintelligible, rather like the little man in our family's His Master's Voice radiogram. Somehow he crammed himself daily into that box when no one was looking, was full of grown-up talk, but every so often with a great whistle started to talk in a strange language, whereupon my father would bang hard on the lid of the box. I was never allowed to pull the webbing away from the place where the sound was and see what he had done. Eventually I began to suspect that maybe there was no one there at all, just a noise. In prayer the noise came from us; in the radiogram the noise came from a nonexistent someone inside. Either way, the noise made little sense.

When I think about the "Gentle Jesus" prayer, I now realise that there was no need for me to comprehend fully what was being prayed. My mother was doing what was required of her, bringing a young child to Jesus. The words she fed into my mouth were, in a sense, formal. After all there was rhythm; and they rhymed so as to be easily memorable. They made sense, to grown-ups. Jesus certainly honoured them, whether or not I had any clue to their meaning. Surely this is true of all "written-out" prayers. They are there for our instruction, as much as their effectiveness in heaven. As for prayer requests, our Heavenly Father understands the needs of His children, whether they can express them in fine phraseology or are limited to infantile gobbledy-gook. All He wants is that we should talk with Him and listen to Him. What Jesus taught us in the Lord's Prayer is sufficient. It can be gabbled off parrot-fashion, or it can be pulled apart and dwelt upon. What matters is the relationship we have to the Person with whom we are conversing.

I understood very little of this as I grew into a teenager. I have told in *Out of the Ark* what little impact the ceremony of Confirmation had on me. I returned home from Canterbury Cathedral wondering what sort of celebrations would turn it into reality. As usual my father turned on the six o'clock news. We ate supper. My mother played the piano and sang a little. Eventually I went to bed. As far as I was aware nothing whatsoever in my life was changed. But a mysterious combination of different kinds of formal prayer, private intercession, pleadings and desperation combined to allow me to know that I had indeed received the Holy Spirit of Jesus, even though the empowering of that Spirit was to come upon me a couple of decades later. Those godparents who had obeyed the injunction of the minister who baptised me in infancy, to make sure that I was taught "all things which a Christian ought to know and believe to his soul's health", were present and praying. Presumably some absent friends were joining them. My own semi-articulate prayer would have contributed, but possibly the most significant prayer was made by someone we never thought of inviting to the service, who was High Church and therefore did not worship with us; she was a retired missionary from India and a woman of prayer, and gave me a prayer card: "Defend, O Lord this thy Child with thy heavenly grace, that she may continue thine for ever; and daily increase in thy Holy Spirit more and more until she come unto thy everlasting kingdom. Amen" (Order of Confirmation, BCP). The Gothic writing was adorned with colourful flowers. It was the only memento I had so I pinned it on the wall above the head of my bed. Months after Confirmation day that prayer card stayed there, mainly because I did not know what else to do with it. So the prayer remains indelibly printed on my memory. I find I have indeed "increased in the Holy Spirit" through no virtue of my own, and I feel thoroughly "defended".

After that experience I was more convinced of the need to try to understand, think through and mean all the prayers I now tried to use in daily devotions. It was hard! The prayers I hunted down in books had been written by pious people, I assumed, and so would probably not suit my condition at all. The language was sometimes archaic and so it was hard to make the prayers my own:

> Prevent us, O Lord, in all our doings, with thy most gracious favour, and further us with thy continual help;

that in all our works begun, continued and ended in thee, we may glorify thy holy Name, and finally by thy mercy obtain everlasting life; through Jesus Christ our Lord, Amen. (Forms of Prayer to be Used at Sea, BCP)

Those not familiar with Elizabethan English may well find themselves at sea! It is so easy to feel like that if you are a child, or if you do not happen to be familiar with Anglican language. Yet the thought expressed — the request that God will precede us in all our activities and that they should all be undertaken according to His will — is wholesome and constructive. If we really mean it when we use it in daily devotions, the whole day's programme could be drastically reshaped. Fortunately nowadays we do not have to be familiar with archaic phraseology. Today's Alternative Service Book asks the Lord to "guide us" instead.

Gradually I grew weary of these formulae. It is difficult to remember, for instance, to ask the Lord to guide everything we do each day, especially if one particular day promises to be exciting and great fun. On that sort of occasion our minds are so full of anticipation that it feels hard to have to remember that we are totally dependent upon God, even for our every breath. We forget that He created the fun as well as promising to be there in time of danger. So formal prayers went out of my mind, except the Lord's Prayer, which I continued to take apart and apply phrase by phrase, to what was going on around me.

The time was ripe for first experiences of another form of praying. During my last year at school a notice appeared on the Sixth Form board inviting anyone interested to come to a prayer meeting. I was puzzled and impressed; puzzled because I could not imagine what point there was in assembling a group of people kneeling in a circle, presumably with their elbows on the seats of their chairs so as to have their backs to one another for privacy; impressed that anyone should announce such a meeting and be prepared to face the scorn with which it was likely to be received by my contemporaries. Only a handful of girls were there, sitting in a circle. I wondered how the leader could possibly have found a prayer handbook that would fit the needs and habits of such a gathering. But all she held was a shabby Bible. She read aloud a short passage from it and began to chat to someone about what she had read, now with her eyes shut; it dawned on me that, although she had not announced the fact, we were all meant to be praying and that I too should close my eyes. Disconcerted, I glanced around to see if any fellow-Anglicans shared my problem of not being able to pray effectively or with dignity unless we had our heads buried and knelt at our chairs, bottoms up. Everyone present had her eyes closed and one by one was joining in the conversation as if talking with a friend and contemporary. There was no recognisable order of priority. Each spoke as and when she felt inclined. Sometimes there were long pauses and I wondered whether I ought to volunteer a remark, just as one feels guilty when a public speaker has finished and time is allowed for questions, and for minutes there is none. But on this occasion everyone appeared to be deep in attentive thought and the "conversation" continued. Just as I was beginning to decide that people like the vicar at home would be outraged at what was going on in this heretical gathering, the session came to a contented conclusion. Heretical or not, it was plain to see and hear: those praying had not merely been thinking about God — they had been chatting with Jesus and He had been awakening responses in them, as if they were children sitting round a table with their adult leader discussing his plans. At first I was suspicious of the informality and the lack of approved, carefully-constructed phraseology; then I too was able to relax into a situation where I could listen and think, even focus my mind on Jesus. Somehow it was a refreshing relief. But . . .

It is amazing how renewal, the baptism of the Holy Spirit

– whatever expression one uses – transforms one's whole experience of life. Somehow, once Jesus has become Lord of every aspect of life, as well as Saviour, then every minute of every day can become saturated with Him. Not that life becomes drearily sanctimonious: quite the reverse; every minute is interesting, every person valuable and someone to be delighted in. It is as if our Lord were looking through our eyes, so that we can, if we will, see life to some extent as He does. That means that prayer is much more a matter of having a private "think" and waiting for the Lord to furnish a reply in one's mind. Provided the "conversation" is focused on Jesus, it is surprising how often the ideas that come into the mind are fresh and entirely in keeping with the essence of the Gospel, the love of God and of one's neighbour; my praying nowadays lacks the querulous and critical doubting which used to be characteristic of it – unless, of course, my old self crawls in to try to make a judgmental come-back. We know we need only re-focus our minds on Jesus and He will renew our whole attitude. Now it is easy to understand how that little group of schoolgirls could look as if they were conversing with Jesus. Most assuredly they were! And all the other ways of prayer are infinitely valuable, according to need and situation: alone first thing in the morning, when using the prayer Jesus taught, is for me the best way of facing the day, applying it phrase by phrase to the situations that probably lie ahead; chatting informally and silently when going about one's business in the course of the day; dwelling on the significant and beautiful phraseology of the liturgy in a great assembly of fellow-worshippers, differences with other denominations forgotten; or just mulling through the events of the day with the Lord, alone or with one's family at night. All forms of conversation with our Lord are a real delight at last.

Once I started to look again at books of other people's prayers, which had once been my sole, very dry mainstay, I could see that reading these was like joining in a printed prayer-meeting with an eternal dimension, since most of the participants were on the far side of death. Sometimes the prayers were in the form of poetry. George Herbert's "Easter Wings" combines so much of adoration with confession and thanksgiving that it constantly challenges me:

> Lord, who createdst man in wealth and store,
> Though foolishly he lost the same,
> Decaying more and more,
> Till he became
> Most poor.
> With thee
> O let me rise
> As larks, harmoniously,
> And sing this day thy victories;
> Then shall the fall further the flight in me.
> My tender age in sorrow did beginne:
> And still with sicknesses and shame
> Thou didst so punish sinne,
> That I became
> Most thinne.
> With thee
> Let me combine
> And feel this day thy victorie:
> For, if I imp my wing on thine,
> Affliction shall advance the flight in me.

Recently I have discovered how truly it is our Lord who initiates prayer in us. Our son Rupert — whose name means "bold adventurer" — had taken himself off on a solo attempt to reach Algeria. He was enjoying a "gap year" between school and university and had already survived a trip with some missionaries who had asked him to help them build an extension to a school in the southern Liberian jungle, quite near the Ivory Coast, once known as the "white man's grave". He had told us of encounters with tarantulas, with a wave-scorpion in his earth loo, with crocodiles and cobras, and with the threats of the bush society, witchdoctors in the jungle who objected to Christian activity. A trip to Algeria should, according to him, be relatively simple. He took with him merely a sleeping-bag, a sheet of plastic, a rucksack with a change of clothing, his father's compass, £80 worth (all he had) of travellers' cheques and his Visa card. He left England early one Friday morning.

On the Saturday night I was suddenly half-awakened by the picture in my mind's eye of seven fiery-eyed and swarthy men, all of whom were very angry with Rupert. It was as if I myself were Rupert and I was very frightened. So, not knowing his exact whereabouts nor whether there was any real cause for anxiety, I asked Jesus to look after our son and turned over to go to sleep. But the men were still there in my sleep, and no amount of garbled half-formulated prayers could dispose of them.

"You're just a silly ole worry-guts," came a voice inside me. "This is nothing but restlessness caused by your need to go to the loo."

Blearily I groped my way to the lavatory. More awake now, I became much more anxious and aware of the need to pray.

"But Lord, I have no idea of Rupert's present whereabouts, let alone whether he's made his way to Algeria yet. However can I pray effectively for him?"

"You can pray in tongues."

So there, sitting on the loo in the middle of the night, I prayed – something. As I stumbled back to bed a cold voice inside me said, "Your prayers are no use at all. You don't even know what you were saying. A fat lot of good it is for someone like you to pray about anything important."

"Where two or three are gathered together in my name . . ." The quotation came gently into my mind. I climbed back into bed, to join a vigorously snoring husband.

"We've got to pray for Rupert."

Snore.

"I said we've got to pray for Rupert."

Snore, accompanied this time by an acknowledging grunt.

"Please, Jesus, look after Rupert," I pleaded, "Amen."

Snore. This time I elbowed Hugh in the ribs. What was the point of going on alone in this? "You must say Amen."

"Wassat?"

I repeated the brief prayer and the Amen.

Silence. "Amen, ple-e-ase, Hugh."

"Amen."

We both turned over and fell deeply asleep.

Eventually Rupert told us what had been happening to him. He had hitched lifts from Malaga and, in the company of two new French friends, had arrived at the Moroccan border. There he was introduced to a group of men, one of whom spoke English. They offered to show him real Moroccan life and to introduce him to "the family". They drove him to a small town well into Morocco and persuaded him to leave his rucksack in a cheap hotel room, handing in his key at the desk. Then they took him up picturesque stepped streets, where there were bazaars. He was particularly fascinated with the beautifully designed cashmere and silk carpets, but of course had no intention of trying to buy one, let alone carry it home. Then they took him to bars where they drank plentifully. Rupert, having last eaten a proper meal with friends in Surrey, confined himself to Coca-cola and, when things grew rough later in the evening, he took one beer. Very gradually he realised that his hosts expected him to return the hospitality.

"I mustn't do this too often," he tried to explain. "I've only got the travellers' cheques I've just been using and they're meant to be a safety-valve in case I'm in difficulties."

"Come on. You must have more money than that!" they remonstrated.

"I assure you I have nothing more, not even in my rucksack."

Suffer Me to Come to Thee 31

"We know what's in your rucksack and you're telling the truth. Look, we're carrying the key to your room with us. You've got nothing in there. So where is the money?"

"This is all I have."

"What is that at the bottom of your pouch? A Visa card. We can all use that. Come on. How about a girl? Would you like one? They help you to relax. Or, if not a girl, how about a fellow?"

Several paunchy middle-aged Moroccans drew around the boy in an inviting way.

"I'm just out of school. I'm nineteen and I haven't come to Morocco for this."

Rupert remembered advice he had received that if ever he was face to face with a gang he should not try to deal with them physically, single-handed. Here in Morocco he had no precise idea of his whereabouts nor, if he were to get away, did he speak the language. So he co-operated until faced with this situation. The men took him from bar to bar, making him sign Visa applications for drinks and women for themselves.

"I can't sign away this money," he protested. "It doesn't exist."

"Your father will bale you out. Come on. Relax." They handed him a dirty old hairbrush. "Tidy yourself up. Reception will never accept your Visa application if you look like that."

Having to brush his hair on command was anathema to Rupert and he protested.

"Perhaps you haven't yet realised; we're armed. The Moroccan Mafia is never unprepared."

As soon as he could Rupert excused himself to retreat to the privacy of the lavatory, so that briefly he could "crack up" in terror. But the gang leader followed him in there.

"If you behave like a little boy, we shall all rape you."

It must have been at that point that I was being invited by my Lord to pray in tongues on the loo at home.

Rupert related in his police report and in his account to his family how he pulled himself together and emerged to face the gang again. They had assumed that he was a courier for hashish and had been puzzled at his failure to mention the matter. Through the international Mafia network they discovered that Saturday night that his Visa account was bankrupt. Frustrated and furious, they drove him along a coast road flanked with scrub and discussed where to dump his body. Something stopped them coming to agreement and so they bolted him in an empty room in a disused house for the rest of the night, with one gunman for company. Next morning Rupert awoke to find that this was no nightmare. He was still in danger of his life. He recommitted himself there and then to his Lord.

"Your dealings with us have been truthful and honest. We had a good night out on the town, thanks to you. The rest was a mistake. We have decided to put you in this taxi, and send you to the border. Here is your rucksack."

Incredulous, Rupert fished out his father's compass to discover the direction in which the taxi was heading. He was indeed being dumped – in freedom!

The mountaineer churchwarden of the "Bah-de-bee" sermon had come a long way. So had I! However I still had not fully learned the humility to come into the Lord's presence in total emptiness, to listen before I began.

4

IN A MYSTERIOUS COMMUNION

"Mum, you might as well let them all into the playroom, now so many of them have been in secretly just for a look. The boys will soon get stuck into the sausages and that won't be fair," sighed a flustered Juliet.

"OK. I'm afraid you'll have to excuse me," I apologised to the last of the ferrying parents. "Thank you so much for . . ." The front door swung closed.

"Right! Let battle com-MENCE!" shouted Rupert, his mouth already full. Girls clad in immaculately-ironed broderie anglaise and velvet did not do nearly as well as Bridget's closest friend Susie. She had arrived well-prepared, in towelling track-suit and bright trainers. Soon the paper party-plates, splodged with mixtures of jelly, crisps and pickled onions, were strewn across the table, abandoned.

The boys were already outside playing football and shinning up our fire-escape. Table fireworks had proved a big disappointment after the splendours of November the Fifth and so posses of young visitors were brewing rival entertainment. It was time to pause and redeploy ourselves.

"Front room, everyone!" I called.

The message spread quickly. Something was going to happen in the front sitting-room. As quickly as they had dispersed they all reassembled.

"Who knows how to play Dead Lions?"

This was a game that had always proved useful when the children needed to calm down, to digest hastily-gobbled food, to recover from injury, to rest from the fray, to stop picking on one another, or merely to recover their dignity and self-discipline. Now three or four co-operative partygoers flung themselves on the floor and settled as if for sleep.

"Good. If you want to join in, just lie down and pretend to be dead."

Everyone flopped so excitedly to the floor that I felt ashamed; I was about to cheat them all.

"Now stay there. No one is going to touch you, but I shall do everything I can to make you move and prove that you are not dead. You'd be best to shut your eyes; then you won't be caught blinking."

A sudden hush fell on the room. A plane could be heard purring through the mid-afternoon clouds.

"Phew! Peace!" I thought. "I do wish I could just leave them like this, creep out and clear up the playroom." At that moment someone sneezed. "You're out, I'm afraid, Vicky."

Vicky jumped to her feet resignedly and started to help me distract the corpses into life.

Suddenly Bridget got up from the floor and declared, "Mum, we're too big for this kid's stuff now. Why can't we play a proper party game? Come *on*!"

In no time at all the partygoers were up, ready to whirl around, competing for prizes, searching for active fun: after all what is the point of having a party if we are forbidden to relate to one another?

I must have been a little like that about corporate prayers at some stage. Before I understood silent meditation I had looked upon it as the children looked on Dead Lions: an unnecessary and boring interlude. My first discovery of its real worth had come much earlier when Rupert was a baby. We were invited to a holiday house-party in Anglesey. The cliff-top views of the sea in all its moods, the silence of sun-bathed gorse and the challenge of gales unrestrained by any land-mass were the essence of that holiday. The house we stayed in had been the holiday home of our hostess's family for many generations. Little had been altered anywhere in the building: the Elizabethan farmhouse-sized kitchen with its Rayburn range was the centre for any warm rendezvous; the bedrooms, spacious and high-ceilinged, were elegant on a fine day, gaunt during a Welsh drizzle; our farming predecessors had gone to bed by candle-light; so did we.

As we were clearing up at the end of a toy-strewn holiday I settled on my knees to brush by hand many yards of sand-encrusted corridor. As I did so the silence and serenity of the place began to influence my attitude, even to that chore.

No longer was I running over the headland in the freedom of the wind, glad to acknowledge the magnificence of the cliff face, wodged by an almighty hand into quartz-laced prehistoric formations and sculpted by the unceasing ocean. Now I was to clear up human mess and should, on a place named appropriately Holy Island, be able to acknowledge Jesus even in this. As I brushed I remembered the *Ancrene Riwle*, the rule of an order of medieval anchorites, which I had come across during my Middle English studies. As a student I had been impressed by the fact that these nuns managed to transform every chore they had to undertake by relating it to some form of devotion. As they knelt on work-hardened knees scrubbing stone floors, it was their rule to sanctify that activity by using the position to remind themselves of their humble, penitent devotion to their Lord.

"It's all very well for them," I remonstrated with the Lord who was drawing me, even in this brushing job, closer to Himself. "They weren't constantly distracted by the demands of small children. As far as I remember they were each allowed to keep one small cat. Silence to them was a blessed time consecrated to you. Silence for me, at least when they aren't tucked up asleep, can only mean that the children are up to some mischief. The anchorites could shut the cat outside. You can't do that with children — not with those cliffs so near."

Through a haze of salt-sand dust I tried to smile up co-operatively to Mary, my hostess, as she went to tackle the bathroom lino with mop and bucket.

"Do you remember those women in the *Ancrene Riwle*?" I grinned ruefully. "I'm trying to think how to apply their prayer-practice to sweeping up children's beach-mess. I suppose they had mops and buckets of a sort — and brooms." I straightened an ache out of my spine and considered.

Mary, unaware of my immediate discomfort, volunteered, "Are you really interested in meditation as they practise it still in religious communities?"

Into my mind crept pictures of sombre-faced solitaries devoting themselves to discomfort in order to "centre down" to the simplicity of silence, the inner man. Too often was I made aware by our children of another "inner man"; feeding time would soon be upon us.

"Not really," I grunted, sweeping a bigger cloud of dust up my nose, into my eyes and down my neck. "I'm just trying to make something positive of all this."

"There's a form of Christian meditation I'm involved in. We meet on a weekday afternoon," persisted Mary.

"No use to me. The children have their naps then," I countered.

"Ideal! My two friends and I will come to you."

So it was that one afternoon, as Juliet and Rupert agreed at least to lie down and be quiet, if not to sleep, the doorbell rang and three ladies of a mature age crept into the sitting-room in silence. Trimming their forms into the backs of their armchairs they sat with their knees together, upright, still and attentive. After a few minutes the leader handed us slips of paper on which were written the thought upon which we were to concentrate:

"I am peace within thee."

In a Mysterious Communion

Then she read aloud a brief exhortation for us to empty our minds, focus on our Heavenly Father, and be filled with His peace. We sat for a period of five or more minutes. Awestruck and interested though I was, my mind flitted into interpretation of one sound after another: passing cars, birdsong, the creaks of an elderly house, the tick of the clock, the swish of a fly hitting the window. I knew that I should empty my mind completely. I tried hard to do so in order to receive the peace. The others held their hands open expectantly. I did the same. The fire settled into a fascinating new log-formation and fresh flames leapt. I closed my eyes hastily; I must concentrate – hard – on being empty. Cars outside were swishing past; my nappies on the garden line would be getting wetter and wetter, soon the children would stir . . .

The leader called my attention back to the matter which should have been in hand.

"Let us be still and bring into the peace the names of those I shall now list. It is important that we do not present to God any prescription, remedy or course of action for those for whom we now pray. He is sovereign. We bring them, names only, into the peace."

I was bewildered. Several of the names meant nothing to me. I was accustomed to the form of intercessory prayer where I thought out, in the Lord's presence, what I could in faith ask Him to do, and what in the circumstances I would do to further the remedy. As it was now, I was in the position of a bystander trying to watch what was happening to someone I had never met; and it seemed to me that nothing particular would happen. Another long silence was punctuated by a sudden snort from someone as a snore got out of hand. I tried hard to relax, to empty myself.

The Beings, as I had christened them, eventually gathered themselves together and silently and unobtrusively departed. At that moment loud "view halloos" could be heard from the children upstairs, indicating that it was time I allowed them to snap once again into friendly, boisterous action. Offers of cups of tea and an interchange of news were clearly inappropriate. The Beings had departed; curiously, their peace remained.

For all my indignation I had learned several new aspects of private prayer and intercession. I noticed that silence could be very noisy, if one allowed one's thoughts to roam freely. As I pondered I realised that the prescribed "emptying" meant a refusal to accept anything of self, self-concern or distracting anxieties about the well-being of things or even of people. An "empty" mind can be extremely dangerous as we can then leave unoccupied space for all sorts of deception, fantasy and falsehood. So it was important for the leader of that Christian meditation group to urge us to allow our minds to be filled with one of the qualities of God. I noticed how gentlemanly is our Lord. He did not in any way obtrude, but was there, waiting to give us of His own personality, fully and freely. If, in the course of receiving, weary souls fell asleep in the luxury of His calming power, there was no condemnation or guilt. If, on the other hand, we were able to let Him discipline our spirits into surrender to His will during the intercessions, then somehow we were in our prayer freeing Him to perfect His purposes for those we named. In a mysterious communion of like minds it somehow did not matter that we did not know the full dimension of each problem nor, in some cases, the person behind the name. Can we mortals ever know someone as thoroughly as the Lord does? Afterwards I learned that several of the people prayed for had been freed of their trouble at the time when we prayed. Others were healed. Some still needed to be "held in the peace".

It was around this time that I was learning about and observing another way of being still and listening while in the company of others. Freshly renewed in the Holy Spirit

In a Mysterious Communion 39

I had attended a healing rally and observed incredulously how Trevor Dearing, the leader, was hearing the Lord about the needs around us. The Holy Spirit's gift of knowledge was in triumphant operation, moving silently among those in the congregation who had stood to signify their need for healing. All anyone was required to do was to focus his whole attention on Jesus, in silence. Gradually those who had been standing had one by one resumed their seats as Trevor received information about their various forms of illness and prayed appropriately.

The Lord works in ways beyond our analysis: sometimes He gives a gift of knowledge, intimately concerned with a person quite unknown to the recipient of the knowledge: at other times, as in silent meditation, those praying know nothing but a Christian name. As the Lord pleases, so He chooses to respond to prayer. It is our privilege that He sometimes allows us to be witnesses to what is happening.

With the loving, intimately concerned guidance of the Holy Spirit of Jesus, silent prayer gradually became a time when I could, as Isaiah did, "hear a word behind me, saying, 'This is the way. Walk in it' ", when I "turned to the right or when I turned to the left" (Isa. 30:21). Jesus was to communicate in that way increasingly, often in proportion to my own emptiness and inadequacy.

Part of the challenge for me was to lie down in my willingness to accept the Dead Lion role: to be at peace, resting in the Lord, digesting all He had already fed to me, waiting.

It is still another matter to forget about oneself *or anyone else* and worship God alone. George Herbert wove together in the intricate pattern of "Easter Wings" an attempt to "sing this day" Christ's victories. He knew that anything man-made is inadequate unless in our feebleness we can graft or "imp" our "wing" on Jesus. In other words all our attempts at worship and adoration are totally inadequate unless, aware of our own sinfulness, we lean totally on Jesus' own love of His Father. And I can only lean or "imp my wing on thine" when the Holy Spirit of Jesus is there to do it all in love, for me.

What use, then, is anything but silent contemplation?

5
JESUS' SUPPER PARTY

Juliet, clean, combed and in her Sunday frock, knelt beside me, staring up, fascinated. Rupert, thirteen months her junior, was holding firmly on to a clump of my long hair as I tried to prevent him from using the altar rail as a baby's gate-vault. The choir was intoning a dour anthem; celebrant and server passed along the row, alternating wafer with blessing as was appropriate to parent and child. Perhaps Juliet was remembering my instruction not to demand a wafer or drink; perhaps she was awestruck by the proximity and swish of liturgical garments.

We returned to the privacy of our pew. A small voice piped into the silence: "If this is Jesus' supper party, why aren't we all enjoying it and being friends with each other? Tell me again why I couldn't have any!"

Those in authority taught that little children should be able to accept the fact that much adult activity must to them seem a mystery. This was certainly so for the Holy Communion. We were not all "enjoying it and being friends" presumably because each of us had come misguidedly to understand that our relationship with God must be restricted to the personal, that our concentration, whether or not we were in a group, ought to be solely and individually on God. Anyone who made Juliet's comment, even in a large congregation, had failed to recognise our "aloneness" and was being childish; anyone who, like me, could not answer her remark simply had not thought deeply enough yet and perhaps was unworthy of being there at all. I thought of the one prayer Jesus taught us, the Lord's Prayer; "When you (plural) pray, say *Our* Father". Why could we not enjoy it as a party and be friends? Why could she not have any wafer or drink? I could not say, "Because it's only for those who have confirmed their baptismal vows." Juliet had many times over affirmed her trust and love for her friend Jesus. She was committed to Him, tried to obey Him and knew how to ask His forgiveness; she readily made friends with Him again and chatted with Him freely.

Skirting Juliet's first question I made an inane attempt at the second.

"You can't have any, because it's for big people only."

However her remark about being friends was honoured within weeks. Communicants returning from the altar rail ahead of our little family cluster were filing soberly down the chancel steps to their pews. A middle-aged widow, warm friend of us all and therefore aware of Juliet's distress, was returning, eyes lowered, and as she drew level with Juliet one eye opened wide and snapped closed like a camera lens, in one straight-faced and shocking wink.

Later, after the Down family had joined us, there was hope that we would be able to worship together corporately in the warm fellowship of God's family. All five children, two Downs and three Allans, were teenagers and committed Christians. Martin was authorised to celebrate Communion, although it was our habit to worship in church with the rest of the parish on Sundays; but we felt that as renewed Christians under the guidance of the Holy Spirit we should as a household be able to learn fresh insights into what Jesus intended by His institution of Holy Communion, His last supper party.

We all agreed to reserve early Wednesday evening as a suitable time to join together for this. Initially it was a struggle. The service was arranged for seven o'clock or earlier, as a follow-through from family supper at six. Cheap

Jesus' Supper Party

telephone time is from six onwards; the children awaited calls to discuss homework or the merits and looks of new boy and girl friends; the adults could expect long-distance calls from friends and family. So the telephone had to be taken off the hook until the service was finished. It lay there buzzing with accusatory indignation until the receiver was eventually replaced.

We wiped the kitchen table down, set a candle in the middle and composed ourselves for Communion. We handed round the Alternative Service Books and waited expectantly. For the first few Wednesdays Juliet, seventeen, fetched her guitar and we sang one or two choruses. Singing brought us together as a warm family. As Martin led us in the Confession I became thoroughly aware of its detailed implications for me. In church I would be able to escape any specific or embarrassing connection with those in nearby pews; in fact no one would have noticed whether or not I joined in the Confession. Few people would even have known who I was. But here, around a table where everyone knew everybody else, we knew, all of us, most of the occasions when each had sinned against the Lord in word and deed. We were all aware of the things left undone, whether it was the washing-up or an important apology; we were not necessarily so clear about who ought to have taken any action. Most of us knew who had done the things they ought not to have done — and most of us knew who was hurting as a result.

The big challenge of such an intimate yet "general" confession always surfaced in my heart: having admitted my sins I expected to be forgiven! But was I prepared freely to forgive everyone around me? Even when they had not apologised?

In a church service the intercessions were made by a member of the congregation on behalf of persons known either nationally or locally. It was sometimes interesting merely to listen and discover how far the official "intercessor" was up to date with the news, or to check whether what we had heard of local gossip bore any resemblance to the truth. Only on the rare occasion when the matter dealt with was of intense importance to me personally could I make the prayer my own, to intercede with my whole mind and heart alongside the person praying on my behalf.

"We ask your blessing on the current Trades Union dispute." Which dispute? I would gnaw gently at the evasive phraseology and wonder whose side the speaker was taking. The list continued at speed.

"For those who are sick in body, mind or spirit. We pray especially for Mary, Jim, Fred, Peter and Jill. Grant them a happy issue out of all their sufferings. Finally, for those who have departed this life . . ."

"Fred," I wondered. "Now can that be Fred Fawkes? He's in real trouble and his whole family are affected. We ought to be praying that he's healed of his brain tumour, that his wife will put up with his tantrums, that the children are reassured. But perhaps it's not that Fred at all. How much does the speaker know about these people? What's the point of a quick list such as that? I've no idea who the other people he's listed are anyway. Now I haven't heard who, if anyone, has departed this life – and it's time to be up and singing the next hymn."

The scene around the kitchen table was, in the end, no great improvement. When the service book provided a slot for intercessions Martin, the "president" of the service, invited us all to contribute. Here there was room to pray for Fred at length. But how much of what I knew about Fred's situation was confidential. Conversely, perhaps others knew much more than I did or were able to pray more wisely. Into the silence someone would drop one brief sentence.

"We pray for Jim."

Now this was provoking. Perhaps I was supposed to know

Jesus' Supper Party 45

Jim and all the facts that related to the necessary intercessions; perhaps those facts were confidential and Jim was to be prayed for only by those who knew; perhaps we were praying with absolutely no facts at all as a basis. (Much the best, some would say, because only the Lord knows which facts matter.) At all events, Jim was not Fred, and that was where my train of thought had been interrupted. Group intercession was no improvement on public intercession. Within the framework of the formal liturgy there is no time or place for one person to persist inordinately on any one theme. On the other hand, within the loving protection of a small community in homely surroundings there is abundant room for friends to implore the Heavenly Father with full hearts, and if necessary at length. The liturgical intercessions throw wide open the scope of our thinking. I began to realise that our domestic prayers, had they been the only form of Communion the household celebrated, would have been extremely limited. They would have had to depend upon how much any of us had listened to or read the news and been out and about in the local community, to learn what matters ought to be prayed about.

In the setting of a kitchen, or even a well-groomed sitting-room, it is hard to clear one's mind and contemplate God in all His majesty.

"We do not presume to come to this your table, merciful Lord, trusting in our own righteousness, but in your manifold and great mercies. We are not worthy . . ." (Prayer of humble access, ASB).

As we listened to those words, all around us were visible signs of jobs half-finished, matters which drew our attention not so much to our own fallibility as to the distraction that as soon as the service was ended we each planned to go about our all too urgent business. We each felt unworthy to be indulging in a communion service when there was so much ordinary work to be done. Prayer felt like a kind of self-indulgence.

Within a spacious building and in the semi-familiar company of fellow-worshippers there is a distancing from everyday life. However dingy the furniture and scruffy the ornaments in a church it is for me much easier to conceive with awe the enormity of daring to approach the King of Kings.

Many church Communion services nowadays make provision for participants to greet their neighbours with a handshake, or families and close friends with a kiss. This may be as cursory as the feelings are remote, but it is an opportunity for reconciliation and restoration of friendship among God's children. Of course within a household there was no need to make the acquaintance of one another; the greeting was acknowledgment of our unity in the love of Jesus, despite our differences. In church it was sometimes a free movement among the congregation so that fresh friendships could be formed; or more often, and perhaps more profoundly, an acknowledgment of unity with all those now absent in the flesh but with us (each so separate and independent in our pews) profoundly in the Spirit. From this experience I have been drawn to realise the presence of myriads of cherubim and seraphim glorifying the Most High God in paeans of praise.

So where is the homely setting of the upper room supper-party celebrated by Jesus before His death? No wonder Juliet, the little girl, could make no connection between that party and the anthems of the impassive choir. No wonder Juliet, the budding adult, resorted at home to her guitar to sing:

> Holy, holy, holy is the Lord:
> Holy is the Lord God Almighty!

The words were the same, but in church the atmosphere was charged with the remoteness of God; in our workaday kitchen we were aware that the same God had become

Jesus' Supper Party

incarnate, that Jesus was among us, entirely compassionate and aware of us, harassed and helpless. He was bringing the bread of His broken, risen life, our one great hope.

It is easy to try to condemn Roman Catholic, Anglican and Methodist liturgies for being too complex. Those of us who are renewed in the Holy Spirit assume that the same Spirit guides each of us into the whole truth, here and now. Certainly the informality of, say, the cookies and coffee Communion I once experienced in a restaurant in the United States, causes me to think again what I understand about the Last Supper. I have attended Sunday services at "independent" churches, during which the bread and the wine are informally distributed to anyone who wishes to take part in the Lord's Supper. Then I scratch my Anglican head and wonder whether I really want to do so since I have in no way got ready. There has been no confession, no absolution – and I feel dirty; no thanksgiving and consecration – and I feel ungrateful, unaware. George Herbert knew the same feeling: "Love bade me welcome: yet my soul drew back, / Guiltie of dust and sinne . . ."

As a little child invited to a party I do need to accept the invitation by saying, "Yes, I admit my sins and need to be cleaned up before I come. In fact I need a new frock." With the simplicity of a child I need to say, "Thank you for having me," and accompany that with a present of some aspect of myself I have always treasured as my own. After that, who am I to demand anything more than to be there, an invited friend at Jesus' supper party?

6

"I SEE'D GOD!"

Late Sunday afternoon in winter was a time for tea and crumpets oozing melted butter; a time for the crackle of a log fire and the weekend paper; a time for cosiness and laughter. But here we were, because the vicar was a friend, inside a stone church in a stone-cold Lincolnshire village, surrounded by flickering candles and the tantalising whiff of pierced oranges. It was Christingle time.

Baby Bridget was thrashing around in her carrycot, hot with indignation and hunger. Juliet stood perched on a hassock, awed at all the tiny lights. She clutched her orange with its solitary candle and eyed the raisins on sticks that stuck out of the orange so invitingly. She made sure that the scarlet sash stayed in place and listened to the explanation.

"I think you've all got an orange now." Geoffrey was a round, funny friend the children knew from holidays in Anglesey. Mary, his wife, had telephoned to invite us all to this afternoon service in Edenham, a village eleven miles from home, where Geoffrey was vicar. "Who knows what the orange stands for?"

"Foreign fruit," piped a small voice.

"Near enough," encouraged Geoffrey.

"Apples is better," growled a voice nearby.

"Not if they're from France," whispered an older lad behind us. Nationalism made sermons spicy.

"The orange stands for the whole wide world. I mean,

the whole round world." Geoffrey glanced down at his own orange candle-holder and adjusted the scarlet sash. "Don't hold the candle near your hair, will you, or we'll have to call the fire-engines."

Up to this point Rupert had been stacking hassocks at the far end of the pew, building a garage for his toy cars while I held his orange. Now he scrambled up the pile to see what was happening. If fire-engines were to be part of the show then the garage could feature too. From the pew-top vantage point he stood and stared, listening, watching and waiting for the beloved siren. Geoffrey was leaning over the pulpit, rotund and sonorous.

"If Jesus is the light of the world, what do you think the red belt stands for?"

Rupert stared into the unlit gloom beyond Geoffrey, into the chancel where marble and alabaster Ancaster ancestors, some of them Highlanders, were poised ready to do obeisance to the King of Kings at the altar. As his eyes adjusted to that half-world he tumbled off all his hassocks with excitement.

"Piffrey, Piffrey!" he shouted to the gentleman in the pulpit so absorbed in his candle.

Geoffrey paused, leaned further over the pulpit towards his friend of seaside adventures and admonished him.

"Shut up, young man."

"Piffrey, I see'd God!"

After the Christingle ceremony was over, the candles snuffed and the raisins gobbled up, Rupert told us what he had seen.

"He got a funny short skirt and he was white – well, nearly white – and he had a long, long knife – and he was big – and he didn't see me cos he wasn't looking."

One Ancaster Highlander ancestor now stood, High and Almighty, experiencing glory unawares, even if only in this toddler's mind.

My friend Mary had fashioned the Christingle candles

"I See'd God!" 51

with infinite care, fully aware of the significance of candle, fruit, sash and orange, probably praying as she worked that the recipients would understand more deeply the purpose of Jesus coming into the world. It was easy enough for a small child to understand at Christmas the fact that a baby had been born in a manger; far more complex to try to explain that the same baby had shed His blood for each person on earth and that He was their enlightenment. Obviously neither young Rupert nor baby Bridget had gained new insights into their candle-stuck oranges. For the rest of us the shed blood and the enlightenment are matters to be pondered for the rest of our lives. Mary's home-made creation still has significance for me, years after the materials she used have disintegrated.

The purpose of the sculptured alabaster statues is harder to discern. For their descendants there will always be a mild fascination in the physique and expression of those ancestors, a fascination tinged with scepticism. What sculptor should dare to depict his deceased subject with anything but the gravest respect, even verging on misrepresentation, if he hoped to honour the dead and retain his job? For the rest of us, we are reminded that important people in centuries past reverenced God.

One branch of my own family belonged in centuries past to the strict Baptist chapel. Consequently my father disapproved of all adornments, vestments and statues as "graven images". He usually worshipped in an evangelical Anglican church, and waged earnest war against any attempt to bring in new-fangled trappings; in his opinion they all verged on Roman Catholic idolatry.

Pictures, stained glass and more especially carved statues are difficult for some to accept. "Thou shalt make no graven image" (Exod. 20:4) has prevented the Amish people of Pennsylvania from depicting faces even on their dolls. (This I find delightful, because of the freedom it gives a child's mind to embroider the situation as it involves the dolls in circumstances both good and bad; but I am not sure whether that is the intention.) However many of us can learn from such pictures and statues, when the printed or spoken word is too boringly presented or hard to understand. Soon after being baptised in the Holy Spirit I was sitting in the parish church ambling through the liturgy and wishing I was at some charismatic gathering with my friends from this particular congregation. I was not listening to the sermon but wondering what they would make of the clapping and tambourine-banging. Just then I saw him: set immobile but vibrant in stained glass in the easternmost window of the south aisle of All Saints Church, Stamford, is a Victorian saint banging his tambourine! The sermon was there for me: each according to his light must give thanks and praise the Lord. Tambourines, or their equivalent timbrels, were popular with King David, with the Salvation Army and with some charismatics. How delighted must our Heavenly Father be! I imagine Him in all His warm-hearted simplicity reaching for His own tambourine in appreciation of the joy all around Him. When His children are doing their utmost, whether as a well-drilled organ-accompanied, harmonious choir or bashing around as best they can on guitar and tambourine, shouting His praises with all their hearts, the Lord's joy and delight must be profound. He alone can judge the sincerity of it all. "Let everything that hath breath praise the Lord," and it does not matter how, provided the praise is sincere and open. That one stained-glass picture had been created to set me thinking.

This must certainly have been the case in medieval times when liturgy and sermon were in Latin. For the whole congregation of lay-people visual aids and teaching in the vernacular must have been the only means of conveying the good news at the heart of Christian living. Nowadays we delight in the childlike pictures in the medieval prayer books, the books of hours. Those pictures, with all their anachronisms – angels playing rebec and lute, Joseph consulting a *mappa mundi* upon the arrival of the three wise men — are what most people once depended upon for information about Jesus. The modern equivalent is perhaps a vivid, felt church-banner with its bright, childlike portrayal of the Gospel as it relates to us today. Many of us no longer read books; television has taught us to understand best an idea conveyed as a picture.

I suppose the difficulty about "graven images" is most apparent when we start to give undue worth to a thing or place, whether it is the building often mistaken as the House of the Lord or the furniture inside. Opposition to the former comes from those who know that the Church is built of human beings and that the Lord is present throughout the universe; opposition to undue respect for sanctuary, statue or table is more difficult to establish. Most of the furnishings of any church were placed there originally either for practicality — the congregation ought to know where to look or where to sit — or for instruction. A statue is only a three-dimensional picture; a table is a place on which to put things, whether those things are vases of flowers or a cross and the bread and wine.

In the end it is our attitudes that have to be sanctified with that love and respect for one another which only the Holy Spirit can give us. I shall never forget my first experience of speaking at a Salvation Army women's rally. When I arrived before the service I was given a warm welcome and some brief instructions. But my guide paused in dismay to point out to me what I had done: I had put my handbag down in order to leaf through the instructions; it now sat confidently on what I was told was the Mercy Seat. Hastily I removed the offender and stared at the bench below. It was made of finely grained, clean-cut pine, but there was nothing whatsoever, except its position, to warn the uninstructed not to approach except in a condition of complete repentance. However that Mercy Seat and my glib desecration of it has awed me for years; very probably because my offence was not so much against the furniture as against my loving, forgiving hostess, a clear channel of her and my Lord's mercy.

It is always thrilling to be present at an adult baptism. When I first attended such a ceremony my old Anglican doctrinal defences were down. Recently renewed in the Holy Spirit I was filled with unaccustomed love, concern and joy for those taking part. However my ignorant, inexperienced old "self" was fascinated by the logistics of the affair, by the surprise of discovering the small swimming pool under the floor just below where the preacher normally stood. All this was new and most instructive because I was puzzled to see both preacher and baptismal candidates dressed in Saturday morning casual clothes. Bath towels abounded. One most significant baptism was that of Geoff, a Jewish inmate at a nearby prison. During his parole weekend he had arranged to be baptised. At his baptismal service he gave an exuberant testimony about his recent healing and his conversion from Judaism. He invited everyone present who had not been baptised as adult believers but who now accepted Jesus as Saviour and Lord to join him in the pool. Several did. The most important person present was one of his prison officers, a Christian who had led him to the Lord and who had been appointed towel-bearer. Perhaps the most striking sight in that whole ceremony was the picture of Geoff, no longer in prison gear nor in Saturday casuals, but emerging from the "drying room" in dark suit and smart tie, the epitome of decent living, still urging others to believe and be baptised. Here were people taking part in a symbolic pageant, acting out a salvation for which no words are adequate.

Still, the Mercy Seat and the baptismal pool are shadows of the truths they represent. My aunt, after her late conversion, tried hard to avoid mere shadows; she travelled all the way to the river Jordan to be "done properly". She believed profoundly in total immersion and was baptised in the Jordan, emerging from the water joyous and triumphant. Meanwhile other coachloads of travellers were receiving a token splash on the forehead, a memento of Jordan, and they hurried along to the next tourist location apparently unaware of the particular significance of that splash.

The validity of the ceremony lies in the heart of the participant. The rest — pine table, miniature pool, smart clothes, even Jordan itself — are symbols. So is there any place for well-crafted statue or church ornament in the life of a renewed Christian? Jesus used anything immediately to hand as a teaching aid: He encouraged us to consider the flowers of the field, the birds of the air, a widow with her farthing, a little child, even the great stones of the temple, and learn from them. These things were not intricate portrayals of something other than themselves: their very essence was enough to give them value to Jesus as teaching aids. Perhaps we should learn from that.

Yet the ancient Hebrew Scriptures describe the intricate craftsmanship that was used in accordance with God's instructions. Exodus records the details of the lampstand to be placed within the tabernacle:

> The base and the shaft of the lampstand shall be made of hammered work; its cups, its capitals, and its flowers shall be of one piece with it; and there shall be six branches going out of its sides, three branches of the lampstand out of one side of it and three branches of the lampstand out of the other side of it . . . Their capitals and their branches shall be of one piece with it, the whole of one piece of hammered work of pure gold . . . and the lamps shall be set up so as to give light upon the space in front of it. (Exod. 25:31–37)

Jesus was regular in His worship in both temple and synagogue. This seven-branched candlestick in the Holy of

Holies was always in the temple, despite the ravages of invasion and destruction in previous generations. How much it must have signified spiritually to Him begins to become apparent in Revelation: "I saw seven golden lampstands, and in the midst of the lampstands one like a son of man" (Rev. 1:12–13). Later it becomes apparent that the "one like a son of man" is indeed Jesus, the one "Who died, and behold I am alive for evermore" (v. 18). He who found it essential to commune with His Father alone in the vast open spaces of the high mountains was also able to "move among" man-made articles of deep spiritual significance.

As a child He had listened to the teachers in the temple and asked them questions (Luke 2:46). As a grown man He listened to His Heavenly Father and did the same (Matt. 26:36–46) in preparation for His own death and resurrection. Perhaps we renewed Christians should, like Jesus, both listen and ask questions as we observe the Lord's teaching aids, both natural and man-made, whenever we find ourselves in a situation of worship.

The Christingle candle was the subject of wondering awe for little Juliet. That tiny flame could have pierced the gloom of the winter afternoon all on its own. The accumulated light created an aura of warmth, fellowship and fun. Before man ever discovered fire God had created patterns of stars and the quiet persistence of the moon in the heavens. (I will never forget Rupert's delight during a long night of travel across Wales, designed to be achieved while the children slept; he observed, "Look, the moon's come with us all the way across those mountains and as far as our seaside!") Light signified a presence as well as guidance. If we are not satisfied with the cool moon, God has made the sun to proclaim in an infinite variety of splendours that although light, guidance, God's magnificent presence, may seem to be overwhelmed by night, there is always a resurrection – on the other side of this world.

The most intriguing symbol is Jesus Himself, God made man, Word made flesh, the supernatural fully explicit in human form, declaring that He, not the candle nor even the sun, *is* the Light of the world, reflecting the glory of God.

7

FOR MAKING ME ME!

Juliet and Rupert came hurrying home from their first piano lesson with a new teacher. Juliet, aged five and a half, could play a tune called "Run and Jump", three notes in a row, followed by the next three and so on up the scale. Rupert had not until that day learned the first thing about the instrument, but he could sing, loudly.

"Did you have a good time?" I asked hopefully.

Uncharacteristically neither of them was interested in what there was for supper, but answered excitedly.

"Yes. She's got a lovely big doll's house and . . ."

"And her biscuits are better'n ours . . ."

"Cos they're choklit, and I playded and playded . . ."

"On the piano, she did, but I went exploring and they've got two pianos in one great big room, and . . ."

"Did you manage to play her piano all right, Juliet?"

"She's got a big, big doll's house," mused Juliet dreamily.

Worried lest neither child had taken any notice of the music instruction, I turned to Rupert.

"Did Juliet play all right, Rupe?"

"Sounded all right from underneath," he conceded.

"From underneath? Whatever were you doing there?"

"It's a grand piano and so Rupert crawled underneath to see how it worked."

"But it don't work from underneath and so she lifted me up so's I could see."

"And me, and it's got hundreds and hundreds of . . ."

"HAMMERS!" concluded Rupert in triumph.

Maggie, that understanding and sensitive piano-teacher, soon became a firm friend. Her husband was a RAF padre who occasionally presided at services in the local Methodist Circuit. One evening Maggie telephoned in considerable excitement.

"It's Pentecost next Sunday and Fraser is to take the evening service at Luffenham Chapel. Do come and support us. Bring little Juliet and Rupert too. It's for all the family."

"What's going to happen, that it's so special?" I pictured Juliet and Rupert at their fidgety worst at a time which was usually reserved for bath-time romps.

"No one knows. Fraser's like that. We'll all have to wait and see."

Our belated arrival at the crowded village chapel caused an embarrassing stir. There were few seats left, in fact none where the children would get a clear view of the proceedings unless they sat on the floor at the front with the local children. They were far too shy for that; and I was too pregnant with the next baby to have room on my lap for both Rupert and Juliet. Eventually the three of us slid on to the deserted organ seat half-way along the wall and surveyed the scene. Maggie, reassuring and friendly, was seated at the piano near her husband. Apart from them we knew no one. Fraser was talking to the congregation.

". . .so we're leaving the organisation of this whole service to the Holy Spirit. Has anyone anything to contribute?"

There was an awed silence.

"Well, we usually read the Bible now," volunteered a steward. "I've prepared today's reading, if you like."

"Go ahead," welcomed Fraser, seated and totally relaxed. "And I see Ros Allan and her children have now arrived from Stamford. You children will have something to contribute, won't you?"

I must have shown on my face how I felt, but Juliet and

For Making Me Me!

Rupert were just staring adoringly at Maggie and had not heard a word.

"Well, I'll give you to the end of the next reading to think of something," announced Fraser briskly. "Shall we move on, then?" He signed to the steward.

"Listen, both of you. What songs do you know?" I whispered with an arm round each child.

"Red and yellow and pink and green," said Rupert in a hoarse whisper.

"We need a Jesus song. Can't you remember any?"

Juliet sidled closer. "If I was a butterfly," she whispered almost inaudibly.

"Thank you very much." Fraser was dismissing the reader.

"Do you know that one, Rupert?" I mouthed.

"If I was a fuzzy-wuzzy bear!" remembered Rupert gleefully.

"Sh-h!" chorused Juliet and I together.

"Now, Ros. What are your folk offering?"

"I've only brought our own two and they're not very old," I faltered.

"All the better. Come out in the front, you two. Maggie will look after you."

Juliet and Rupert clambered over the organ seat and the knees of the adjacent congregation and trotted down the aisle to their friend at the piano. There followed a long whispered consultation and a few very private hums to the pianist.

"Come and look at everybody and sing them your song, then," encouraged Fraser.

I noticed how muddy Rupert's trouser knees were, how lop-sided Juliet's coat. In a tiny voice, knees squashed together in dismay, Juliet piped a little tune. Suddenly it was amplified firmly and accurately by her brother.

"But Oi just fank you, Father, for making me me!"

I have never been forgiven for that episode. There have

since been occasions when the whole family has been invited to Christian celebrations and I have been reproached with:

"No, don't let's go to that. Mum'll volunteer us."

"Yes. She'll tell them I'll play a trumpet tune and you accompany on your cello!"

"That'll stop anyone at all going next time they have anything."

"And what's the good of that? Don't let's go!"

The meeting in the chapel had indeed been a disaster for our family. I have wondered since what anyone else there made of what was supposed to be the Holy Spirit's guidance. Certainly in our own panic we had neither prayed nor tried to listen. We had not even heard what the reading was, but I expect it was from the first part of Acts 2, when the Holy Spirit came with tongues of fire upon the disciples in the upper room. They were immediately filled with great power and began to declare what great things God had done. To this day I am not sure what Rupert thought about his Heavenly Father making him him; but I do know that throughout his life I have said Amen to that! The creation of any baby, any new person, is always a miracle. Of course the wonder of a mother at the individual who was once a part of her is not surprising; but what is worth pondering is the fact that, whether or not we were aware of Him, the Holy Spirit was indeed at that chapel meeting, inviting us each to recognise the miracle of our own creation. The invitation came by way of the unskilled mouths of young children.

It is interesting to think about the way our music may or may not be pleasing to our Heavenly Father. After all, we are His children, all delightful to Him, whatever noise we make, provided we sincerely intend to worship and praise. Well into adulthood the word "worship" had for me overtones of solemnity, sad dignity and smart clothes, very little to do with joyful acknowledgment of a truly loving Father. The only songs worthy of such ceremony were those found in *Hymns Ancient and Modern* or the *English Hymnal*. Most of the ones I had to sing in early childhood were sung more and more slowly, as verse succeeded verse; initially the organist waited for the congregation; thereafter members of the congregation slowed each other down so that the organist could keep up. Eventually the concept of attributing worth became clear as an interpretation of the true nature of "worth-ship". There were ecclesiastical advertisements for new hymns to be submitted by people who could write poetry. I was awed. After all, many of the names already included in *Hymns Ancient and Modern* were those of eminent writers: William Cowper, John Henry Newman, Charles Wesley, Addison and so on. I wondered whether the Poet Laureate would be commissioned by the Queen to contribute a hymn. No lesser person would be worthy to write in such form for such an established publication.

The word "praise" has worried me for many years. Even after I had been renewed in the Holy Spirit I could not conceive how anything any mortal sang could be fitting "praise". The very word suggested patronage, "Well done this time God!" God the Creator, whose mighty hand had slung into place every star and planet, every mountain, waterfall and glacier, God the deviser of million upon million of individual sunsets and sunrises, could not be appreciated critically as if He were one of us. I was particularly awestruck at the way rare mountain flowers and exotic deep ocean fish come into being, thrive and perish without man's awareness, entirely for God's good pleasure. How could any "praise" be fitting? We ourselves exist only in accordance with His great plans; time is only a relative way of estimating the passing of events. However could such a God need praise from us, His creatures? "He is not far from each one of us, for 'In him we live and move and have our being'," said Paul in his sermon on the Areopagus, quoting one of the Greeks' own poets, Epimenides (Acts 17:27—28). I am reminded of a microscopic view of the millions of atoms, all in intricate dance around each other, which consitute a fragment of matter. We must be like those atoms in relation to our Creator. The only piece of music which expresses this to me is a fugue, part of a Bach cantata which I once sang in Worcester Cathedral. The chins and eyebrows of every singer bobbed up and down in concentration as the semi-quaver wove from tenor to soprano, contralto to tenor again, thence to bass, round and round, in and out, theme upon theme, until all the strands were finally bound together in one great harmony. Here was at least an attempt to grasp the concept of our interdependence and of mankind's very existence taking form only within the Person and will of God. How can atoms such as we ever "praise" God?

Yet David enjoins us in his psalms to bless the Lord and to praise Him. I began to gain some insight into this when I looked at the words "magnify" and "exalt". We surely can play no part in making God bigger, "magnifying" Him, nor in pushing Him up higher, "exalting" Him! It is our own thinking that has to be expanded and elevated. I have to begin to conceive of a Lord who is vaster and more magnificent than I can fully realise. So when we "bless" Him we can begin to try to will Him to be fully satisfied and delighted; when we praise Him we can begin to express our wonder at what He is doing.

Recently I have become much more fully aware of the way in which our Heavenly Father delights in everything He has made. The first few chapters of Genesis are laced with the words, "And God saw that it was good." The fact that He wants to share that delight with me, that His Holy Spirit is highlighting creation in ways where I can at last be aware of its intricacy and beauty, is overwhelming. "He walks with me and talks with me upon life's narrow way" sing the Salvationists; He the Creator and Director of all the stars in the Milky Way makes Himself available for conversation even with me.

For Making Me Me!

"I follow, I follow, in gladness to meet thee, / and hold thee in sight, my life and my light." When this aria from Bach's *Passion according to St John* is sung by a pure treble voice, on my behalf, I can begin to receive whatever my Heavenly Father has to show me. He does indeed walk with me and talk with me. But when I was not renewed in the Holy Spirit there was no way in which I could find spiritual value in anything as humdrum and singable as the Salvationist hymn. Praise, fellowship and conversation with the Lord had to be expressed in the most professional way, not by incompetent me but by someone skilled who could express what I felt. There is a dimension in the renewed Christian life which can benefit from this approach, so familiar to the Roman and Anglo-Catholics: our minds can indeed be elevated by high praise expressed in ways which cause us truly to "magnify" the Lord. Just as singing in tongues can lift the human spirit almost to the threshold of heaven, so exquisite singing in any language can inspire us to worship.

All the same Jesus does indeed "walk with us and talk with us" with the informal jauntiness of the hymn, as we go about our daily business. If we will but notice, He is extremely close beside us "upon life's narrow way". The narrowness is in the now non-existent gap between Him and us. "I in them and thou in me" (John 17:23) was Jesus' prayer to His Father on our behalf. We need to have some easy form of expressing our love of this intimate Lord. The plea decades ago for new hymns and songs has been answered in an abundance, not of long, ponderous hymns, but of easily-learned choruses, mostly Scripture-based and amazingly well known to charismatics worldwide. However some of us in the Renewal Movement are inclined to draw aside from anything classical or composed by someone who does not profess to be a committed Christian.

I am not sure what Handel would have made of the Charismatic Movement. John Wesley may have been "strangely warmed", probably in Handel's old age. However some divine urge must have empowered Handel to compose the *Messiah*. The choral society to which I once belonged had overcome most of the hazards of learning the notes and increasing the pulse of this work so that it made sense, ready for a Christmas performance. The orchestra had been assembled for the final rehearsal. All was at last beginning to take shape, even to the seating arrangements. Until then, we had tangled our way through most of the more complicated passages, but had usually come to some sort of unification over the passage: "And his name shall be called Wonderful." Once the orchestra was there, we began to look upon the prospect of a concert seriously. At the final afternoon rehearsal there were even a few members of the public chatting surreptitiously while we received our final briefing. It was as we sang that passage that it took life.

The drums rumbled: "And his name shall be call-ed . . ."

And the trumpets clamoured: "WON – derful! COUN – sellor! The mighty GOD!"

"The everlasting Father, the Prince of Peace!" offered the singers, at last able to hear themselves again.

We sat down, bubbling with excitement.

"Isn't it thrilling to be able to shout all that glory at Christmas and really mean it?" I enthused to my neighbour.

She was looking anxiously towards her son, who had been contentedly playing with his felt-writers until the recent explosion of sound.

"Don't know what Alex is thinking of this. But he is at least smiling. He's tried the Salvation Army Sunday School, but couldn't cope with it. Not with his Dad as he is."

"Why? Doesn't his Dad approve of Christian things?"

"Fred? You must be joking," she snorted. "He's coming tonight. Don't know what sort of comments I'll get afterwards. He's a Muslim. Dunno what he'll make of this 'Everlasting Father' stuff."

For Making Me Me! 67

"What do the children make of their Dad, or of your singing *Messiah*, for that matter?"

The orchestra was receiving last instructions. We would be mustered again shortly.

"The others are grown up. One daughter's a Moonie; the other belongs to the Children of God. They couldn't care less about all this; not that they'll know about it. They live miles and miles away."

There was no time for more. We were about to sing again, this time about the "multitude of the Heavenly Host praising God and saying, 'Glory to God in the Highest, and peace on earth, goodwill towards men' ". My neighbour told me afterwards that she was a Spiritualist. She soon became a good friend and a keen borrower of Good News books. Handel had done his stuff in evangelising the choral society!

The triumphant blast of praise had thrilled or shaken us all. But in the months of rehearsal leading up to Christmas our spiritual food had consisted chiefly of meaningless mumble as we groped to find the right notes. It is during times like this that one begins to discover the value of plainsong, especially when it is enunciated by others. When I first heard the expressionless intoning I was irritated. It seemed to me hypocritical to say − or sing − words of praise or woe without any indication of understanding or emotion. Why did they concentrate only upon their elocution and purity of intonation? Where was the feeling?

"They are singing most beautifully," remarked a friend. "I can really worship while I listen to Gregorian chant."

"Half the time I can't even hear what they're singing," I protested.

"Does that really matter?" demanded Elizabeth. "The idea is to worship in spirit. Words are inadequate sometimes."

I was unimpressed and said so. I needed the inspiration of words to focus my thinking. Or so I thought.

Years afterwards, renewed in the Holy Spirit and visiting

Malling Abbey, I was able to listen to plainsong chant with new ears. This was partly because I had already benefited from much prayer made on my behalf by the Benedictine nuns. I had corresponded with the now retired Mother Abbess and knew the deep wisdom of her advice. The nuns were mostly out of sight, although I could occasionally glimpse the white veil of a novice. The words were again indecipherable unless one happened to be familiar with what was being sung. But on this occasion I was alone. My reactions did not matter to anyone but the Lord. The nuns were singing on my behalf, and they were praying. I started to share in the prayerful atmosphere by concentrating all my attention on the Lord. The music was ethereal. The nuns were doing all the work. I was here on retreat. Nothing whatsoever was required of me. That was a strange sensation, and hard to accept. Gradually I became aware that all I had to do was allow myself to be cherished. For the first time I was able literally to "rest in the Lord and wait patiently for Him" to indicate His will for me, if and when He so wished. It was an occasion of personal ministry to my soul, with no evident human intervention, and it was very good! For the nuns this was an occasion of disciplined worship. I have no idea whether any of them was aware of my presence in the side-chapel. Their concentration and mine was on God alone, but the plainsong was the vehicle of ministry.

This kind of worship is akin to singing in tongues. When that happens those involved abandon themselves to the Holy Spirit and allow Him to have His way. The result is as beautiful as my friend Elizabeth had described Gregorian chant. The result is often ministry or prophecy. The two forms of worship are very close when carried out in sincerity of spirit, although they are apparently so different. In both there is expression beyond words, of emotions, of attentive oneness, of glory.

C.S. Lewis entitled one of his books *Out of the Silent*

Planet, presumably in protest that we are the only part of creation which does not make music to the Lord. However we are beginning to learn that our Heavenly Father does accept all expressions of love, however clumsy. The informal fellowship of praise and worship, of savouring the wonder of all that God is doing, is echoed movingly in Benjamin Britten's *Rejoice in the Lamb*. As the "Hallelujahs" flow quietly from one being to another, it is as if the Father Himself is so delighted with the celebrations that He too reaches for His harp: "Hallelujah, hallelujah from the heart of God". It is to our own loss if we charismatics cannot savour the beauty of this kind of music and the new dimension it gives to our concept of our loving Father. It is clear that He has the same delight that any father has in children who are doing their very best to sing sincerely and with joy. The best way of sharing the fun is to join in!

8

AIRING THAT TEA-BAG

A figure strolled down the garden path. A bright but ragged tee-shirt showed every now and then beneath the mud-stained jacket; trouser-rips revealed sturdy, well-muscled legs; there was the sound of lumps of stone and mud being kicked off mountaineering boots and the regular thud as their wearer bounded upstairs. Soon the house throbbed to *Dire Straits* and *Lynrd Skynrd*. Rupert had come in.

When our two families were living together it was always advisable to stay well clear of the kitchen until someone pointed out to you that, since you were "on cooks", you had better start taking action before James, the grandfather clock in the hall, politely but firmly announced to eight other ravenous people, "Food-time-has-come-at-last!"

The kitchen door burst open. "What's for supper?"

"Can I look?"

"No one's even laid the table."

"Whoever's responsible for this? It looks disgusting."

"Smells exotic to me," purred Hugh, encouragingly rubbing his hands. "Should we be eating so very well?"

Rupert strode in.

"Have you thought of getting some decent trousers?"

"These are my favourites. Just leave me alone. Masks. You all want me to wear masks!"

Juliet and Kate whirled in, dressed for going out later.

"You look smart, Katie."

"Do I? It's Dad's old clerical shirt."

"Found this in the jumblie at the Darby and Joan. It's a Laura Ashley and so I'll probably flog it again," mused Juliet, spreading out a dress for us all to see. "Do you like this gigantic sweater! Size 42, 50p."

"I do wish whoever last used my preserving pan for tie-dyeing would get rid of these horrid purple stains round the handle."

"Sorry, I'll do that after supper," apologised Bridget. "But have you seen what I'm making out of Mum's old sheet? It's a skirt with a really different kind of hem — lots and lots of points. Will someone show me how I can hem points after supper?"

"By the way, where *is* supper?"

James the grandfather clock had been too efficient with his chimes so one of the "on cooks" pair hastily drew our attention outside.

"Whatever's that tiny packet pegged all alone on the clothes line, sort of muddy brown and faded?"

"That's for after-supper drinks. They're on me," volunteered Rupert. "It's one of the tea-bags carelessly left in the teatime pot. I'm airing it to please Dad. Recycling or conservation. Which is it, Dad?"

Part of the challenge of living together in one household was to see whether we could survive materially. Each of the adults was working unsalaried in some capacity for the Good News Trust; the children were at school or about to start at university and enjoyed each other's company as friends. Our reactions to the challenges about food and clothing were varied: some were extremely fastidious about the kind of food we ate; some relished the achievement of producing something from nothing; some, like Hugh, were uneasy at any sign of extravagant living; we were all astonished and delighted at the good things that the Lord provided, often without our even noticing!

It was Rupert who underlined Hugh's anxiety about suspected lack of frugality. The Good News Trust is a charity. No requests for money or gifts are ever made because, as everyone could confirm from experience, the Lord is the mighty provider. He alone nudges His people into giving what they can, when they can. However we can assume that the gifts are given primarily to provide the small library vans buzzing around the countryside, the office equipment necessary to administer this network, the stationery and photocopying materials for producing practical Bible Studies for house-groups. Certainly many of the gifts received were — and still are — for the "maintenance" of those who work full-time for the Good News Trust. But how should we, as renewed Christians, use the resources we had?

Hugh's anxiety is that we should not spend, eat or clothe ourselves so lavishly that we have nothing left to give to others. Freely we have received, freely we should give (Matt. 10:8). How that works out in practice I suppose is different for all of us. The whole world stands in awe of the example set by Mother Teresa and her Sisters of Mercy; they are in direct succession to countless communities who have set the example of living in complete poverty. We learn from them how at least to begin to die to self; some teach, some devote every working minute to prayer, others, like Mother Teresa, work and nurse among the poor. They do not necessarily give in kind what they have received. Nor, when we think about it, did Jesus. Many gifts to Christian groups are given in order to enable them to live as Jesus did: sometimes without anywhere to call home; dependent upon others from time to time for the wherewithal to live; but always fit, always strong enough and sufficiently equipped to go about our Heavenly Father's business competently and serenely. Mother Teresa lives as, and moves among, the poorest in all India; but, thanks to God's provision, she is able when necessary to travel and to give surgical or medical help to the sick. In order to do this she herself must be clean, clothed and adequately fed; when she is ill medical help as well as prayer is available. As with everything concerning the work of God's Holy Spirit, the vow of poverty must be laced with love, not least for the person undertaking the vow!

Health "freaks" would warn us about the dangers of drinking a cup of tea. Rupert had not hung out the tea-bag to dry in mockery of tea. After all it is still supplied as a comfort to people in hospital or involved in an accident or just tired, as some of us usually are. He was more concerned to highlight the danger of attempting to be frugal with something which is useful, cheering and an encouragement to continue working. In the end we were all in agreement that we should spend and eat enough to ensure the health and strength needed for getting on with the work we had to do, and getting on with it as well as we possibly could in order to give God some glory.

The clothing issue has all sorts of subtle connotations. No one can avoid the implications of what they wear. Jesus had some scolding words for people like Dives, the rich man who went around in fine linen while the dogs licked the sores of the poor man at his gate; he also blazed with anger at the Pharisees who sauntered around wearing phylacteries and prayer-shawls. In the first story the rich man had no right to dress sumptuously himself while others nearby were in extreme hardship. In the second the Pharisees were hypocritically proclaiming their own righteousness by the particular adornments they wore, while knowing they were leading many away from recognising their Messiah.

We Christians carp at one another where we could be learning. Some of us complain when our friends attend church dressed as if for a royal occasion. "They haven't thought how off-putting that must be for those who like to praise the Lord in their old blue-jeans and anoraks." We, who are thrilled to bits and rush out to buy a new suit, dress or at least a hat when we are invited to a wedding, scowl and mumble, deaf to the suggestion that we should wear our best when entering the presence of the King of Kings.

Airing that Tea-Bag

Conversely renewed Christians joyously bounce along to worship in bright sweaters, even rainbow braces, oblivious of the fact that some of our fellow-worshippers prefer to "cast their golden crowns upon the glassy sea" only metaphorically; anyway they could not afford the braces!

As I write this I have today come away from a funeral service in a respectable Anglican church. The person who has gone to glory was a wonderful witness to God's power in her life. As I stepped out into the misty gloom of a November Monday afternoon a voice hailed me.

"Can't go away without greeting our Ros, even if she does pretend not to know me!"

I turned, slow to recognise the speaker. I had at first assumed he was a Labour Party candidate off to some local conference. Then I saw it was my ever-radiant friend Peter dressed in his uttermost funeral best: a brown suit with a scarlet shirt and matching silk tie.

"Took the afternoon off work for this," he grinned. "Told the boss I needed time off to attend a resurrection."

So why did Rupert decide he would go around in torn, muddy clothes so as not to be "wearing masks"? He knew that the adults in the household expected him to look "decent", clean and well-mended. He was physically so well-built that his whole presence declared good health. The mud on his jacket spoke of tree-climbing adventures in nearby quarries. The torn tee-shirt and trousers suggested plenty of vigorous exercise. Had he brushed his jacket down and ensured that his trousers and tee-shirt were in one piece, no particular message would have been conveyed. As it was I think he saw no connection between his life as an adventure-loving lad and the necessity to appear always clean and respectable. As a Christian he found a distinct advantage in looking scruffy. He knew that expensive clothes spoke volumes and were likely to convey to his particular brand of acquaintances the lie that in order to follow Jesus you must look smart.

In our more ascetic moments some of us decline good food because we think it important to fast. Clearly Jesus found value in this: "*when* you fast"; but taught us not to flaunt our "righteousness" before others: "anoint your head and wash your face, that your fasting may not be seen by men but by your Father who is in secret" (Matt. 6:16—18). The Roman and Anglo-Catholics have demonstrated to us the importance of the discipline of fasting. This discipline can be of value to our prayer-life, because we are told that the mind is most receptive when the stomach is empty. We can hear the Lord most clearly when our minds are not occupied with food preparation and our bodies with food digestion. Moreover we have far more time free to be about our Heavenly Father's business! A small material corollary is that food not eaten is food that can be given.

In a mysterious way fasting with a purpose, as it is carried out, for instance, by Mother Basilea Schlink's community, is important to God's plans. That Darmstadt community of nuns spent much time in repentance, prayer and fasting and, we learn in Basilea Schlink's *Realities*, by those means managed to effect the diversion of a motorway whose course had been designed to run through their midst! We in the Good News Trust have tried to emulate this kind of fasting. When we have known there is a real need for outreach into the community of some particular area by means of a Good News van, we have fasted and prayed for the main part of a Friday. During one late evening £500 in used notes plopped through the letterbox on to our doormat in answer to a specific prayer! No one but ourselves had known the content of that prayer nor of many others, similarly answered since. The purpose of the fasting is far more important than the practical way in which it is observed.

"Is not this the fast that I choose," says God through Isaiah, "to loose the bonds of wickedness, to undo the thongs of the yoke, to let the oppressed go free, and to break

Airing that Tea-Bag

every yoke? Is it not to share your bread with the hungry, and bring the homeless poor into your house?" (Isa. 58:6–7). Once we have brought the hungry in to share our bread, assuredly the fast must end! After all fasting is the opposite of feasting. That does not apply solely to food, either. A feast is a time of celebration, of making our guests aware of the joy we share in their company.

Once, before I was renewed in the joy and love of Jesus' Holy Spirit, dreary old conscience insisted on my attending a Bible Study at the home of my brother's doctor friend. It had been a hard day of teaching for me with little time to eat; now the weather was squally, and I felt dutiful but dull as I pedalled my way across Bedford wishing my conscience would have let me stay at home by a warm fire with an exciting book and some Mozart.

Wind-buffeted and tousled, I searched for somewhere to hang my anorak. The hall was spacious, almost a room in itself, hung with oil-paintings discreetly lit by spotlights. I was ushered into a thickly-carpeted lounge, where flowers hung heavily over mahogany tables. I sank into silk swansdown cushions on a settee where I could easily have fallen asleep before the great log fire, were it not for the freshly-ground coffee and florentines being passed on rare china. That evening's study was based on the passage in Matthew's Gospel, "Do not lay up for yourselves treasures on earth, where moth and rust consume and where thieves break in and steal . . . For where your treasure is, there will your heart be also" (Matt. 6:19–21).

"However can your friend live like that and yet talk of those things? It doesn't make any sense," I challenged my brother, who had invited me.

"The question is, were you comfortable? Did you feel welcome?"

"Yes, of course I did. It was wonderful after the day I'd had, but . . ."

"That is the whole purpose of Chris's ministry; to

welcome a stranger in the most comfortable way he possibly can, and to give him − or her in your case − rest. When they're on their own he and his wife live frugally enough, but if they are to love their neighbours really as themselves they'll give you what amounts to their idea of a treat."

Frugal living where others benefit in deed!

That is the example set too by the Benedictines, whose plainsong chant I have already mentioned. The retired Mother Abbess at St Mary's Abbey, Malling has prayed for us and corresponded for several years. When I went there for my first retreat I had an appointment to meet Mother Osyth during the visit. As I drove into the village of West Malling I grew more and more timid. What if I was expected to attend offices in the middle of the night? If everyone there was silent, how would I find my way? Was I really going to be at peace in a convent where everyone was absorbed in silent personal contemplation of our Lord all day and all night too? The cheerfully floodlit hotel on the entrance to the village looked inviting; if I was unable to find the abbey, then I could book in there quite happily for one night and then buzz off home in the morning. The thought of the reaction of loving Mother Osyth, and the ribaldry I would have to face from the household once my failure became known made me wind down the passenger window of the car.

"Could you tell me how to find the abbey?" I asked a late-night shopper reassuringly weighed down with domestic goods and a toddler.

"It's back down that lane, behind a closed gate. The driveway will be dark at this time of the evening. Are *you* going to stay there, then?"

Her astonishment was a little irritating and spurred me on to fulfil what I had undertaken.

The wicket gate stood firmly bolted in a stone arch. I pressed the bell once, half hoping no one would be within earshot so that I could justify my failure to arrive. Then

Airing that Tea-Bag

a light flickered all around the edge of the oak slab, a bolt was slung back and a little nun shone her torch first at my luggage and then up at me.

"Why, you must be Rosalind!" She flung her arms around me in a hug of welcome. "Come in, my dear, and I'll take you to the Guest House."

Soon I was sitting alone, eating a bowl of warm baked beans and fragments of home-made brown bread. More bread, butter, home-made jam, tea or coffee and a bowl of fresh fruit were available. The silence seemed, at first, total. Then my ears grew more accustomed as the stillness was fragmented by the fresh babble of a stream beneath the window. What was expected of me? Who would be the first person I must get to know? I cleared my own plates and went to my room, passing no one on the way. The room was cosy; a bright Welsh blanket beckoned towards bed. It was only half past eight. I sighted the day's programme, or was it a menu? It was a list of services I could attend if I wished, and of meals I could take if I wanted them. Compline was already past and I had eaten. I waited attentively for a summoning or concerned knock on the door. Nothing. If I wanted company where could I go? What of those who had brought nothing to read? Then I remembered the spacious sitting-room I had passed, studded with armchairs flanked by discreet collections of books both Christian and secular. What was required of me? After all I was supposed to behave suitably in this guest house. Nothing. Then it hit me. I was, when I looked at the matter, exhausted. I could, with offence to no one at all, go to bed cuddling the hot-water bottle provided, and stay there until I awoke.

As I dozed off to sleep I looked around me. The cross above my bed was hand-carved. The thick Welsh blanket was hand-woven, reversible, bright. Even my hot-water bottle had a hand-knitted scarlet cover. Neither of these was necessary because the room was centrally-heated. A hot bath awaited me at any time of day or night.

Next morning a note awaited me: "Mother Osyth will be brought to meet you at 2 p.m. at St Martin." This was a small interview room just inside the main abbey. In some awe I came to the main entrance, wondering where, whether and how I should interrupt the silence of that ancient building. I had no need to worry. A joyful welcome awaited me. The nuns had been on the lookout and opened a side door as soon as I arrived. With a glad hug Mother Osyth introduced herself and ushered me to a deep armchair. "Bring it nearer the radiator, my dear, then you'll be really warm."

I looked around to discover with dismay that there was only one soft chair. The venerable ninety-year-old retired Mother Abbess and her blithe young escort arranged themselves on small, upright hard chairs and leant eagerly forward, attentive to their guest.

It was here that I was to learn the true joy of living in complete simplicity so that others can be blessed. The clue was in Mother Osyth's farewell. She planted the sign of the cross on my forehead and blessed Jesus-in-me, for "He is all and in all." Jesus came that we might have life, and have it more abundantly. The abundant living for these Benedictine nuns consisted of living within the perfect will of Jesus. They joined their Creator in making the finest and most wholesome. Everything they did or made was given in love to those they encountered, whether it was the beauty of a skilfully-channelled brook, or the crisp warmth of a fresh-baked roll. Everything drew our attention to the abundant love implicit in creation; as they welcomed each of us as vehicles of Christ, so we began to be introduced to the joy and love of Jesus all around us.

Once we can recognise this abundance of life with Jesus, then there can be no restraint in keeping festival. Where Jesus is, there is love. Frugality becomes a means through which those around us can be fully satisfied in everything that they need. Since we are each involved in being one of

Airing that Tea-Bag

"Those around us" each in the end is fulfilled in love and a recipient of joy.

When the Down family lived with us they established a custom which as a family we intend to keep a Christmas tradition all our days, even if it is uneconomic and inconsistent with the tea-bag mentality! Towards the end of Christmas day the candles on the tree are lit, the electric lights switched off. Each of us picks a candle to represent ourselves and there is a fascination in seeing whose light lasts the longest. We hum carol themes gently round the dying fire and ponder the significance of the day, the meaning of each light, the reality of Jesus, the Light of the world. The candles which stand nearest the draught, perhaps the lives which are most open to the Wind of the Spirit, burn most brightly but erratically; those in more secluded positions, behind the tree and almost unseen, burn steadily, providing reliable light and even warmth. But each candle gives light; each represents a person; each in some way reflects the True Light of the world; each one matters and is loved.

All candles together are giving back to God in silent worship what He, the Light of the world, has given us in abundance. In worship and self-giving there can be no frugality.

9

A BUS-LOAD OF BOFFINS

Bridget was absorbed in creating a story, using the round-headed, stubby wooden figures of the passengers on the wooden bus. This was a pull-along contraption that had once taken pride of place among Penelope's toys. Penelope, not three years old, and our first-born daughter, had died soon after her sister Juliet was born. I had made a tapestry cover for a long stool, showing what colourful part could be played by each passenger in time of crisis. The designing and stitching had taken months of concentrated effort; but all our children had independently concocted their adventures for the bus passengers. It was not until they had outgrown the bus that they actually studied what was woven into the tapestry stool.

This time the bus had overturned, the dog having tripped over the pull-along string. Bridget was supervising the chaos. One of the passengers had been pulled from underneath the bus and was lying there, still solidly round and rosy. This was blonde Milly. Rose, her raven-haired travelling companion, was having hysterics, fussing over Milly.

"I telled you somefing was goin' to go wrong. Now you've had an all-fall-down!" squeaked Bridget.

Two wooden-faced gentlemen were commiserating with one another well away from the "accident".

"I wanted a drink-of-rosehip. And now look what's happened. They'll have to pick Milly up, Albert, or I'll never be give it."

"It's my poorly knee that hurts," grunted Albert. "Fat lot of good these Mummies are once they get fussin'!"

The fifth passenger was at last extricated from the rubble, a stolid-looking policeman, much of whose navy-blue had been rubbed off by overtime duty. However his nose and cheeks were still rubicund.

"What's ben going on here?" He stumped over a mess of bricks and Lego. "I'll have to take-yer-name-and-address, I s'pose," he offered the recumbent Milly.

Bridget squeaked her own name and address as fast as she could, on behalf of Milly, who happened to have rolled over with her back to the interrogator, while Rose hobbled up to the two doleful and deprived men.

"Come and help, please, you boys. Milly's all-fall-down!"

Albert and Fred stared blankly straight ahead. "We can't. We're busy," declared Fred.

Then Milly saw the clergyman. He had rolled in another direction altogether, but could be fetched. Rose was walked across to him.

"Milly's hurting. Please come and pick her up and give her a plaster. She's all-fall-down! So is the bus! Oh, dee, dee, dee!"

The clergyman was brought at a run to the scene of the accident. All he could be made to say was a bland, "Blessings on you, my child." Then he just stood and stared. In the end it was Bridget herself who righted the bus, steadied the passengers as they all climbed aboard and muttered as an afterthought, "Blessings on you, my child."

If educational psychologists were to analyse this they might have plenty to say about a child's attitude to authority figures: to the clergy, the police, towards people who assumed responsibility, even towards those who refused to accept any responsibility at all. However they would be wrong. Those bus passengers had lost half their paint because they had all been involved in deeds of derring-do. At some point each had been brave, cantankerous or loving.

A Bus-Load of Boffins

The one phrase which came invariably from the clergyman alone was "Blessings on you, my child."

Perhaps the children had heard something like this at Communion or when they interrupted adult conversations with the harassed vicar as we left the church on a Sunday. There was a peremptory dismissiveness in the tone of the wooden clergyman. Perhaps that was to do with the final blessing at the end of a service, the code words which signified release. At any rate clergy were, like the police, type-cast. That is true of children's stories and television. It must be that we adults have encouraged this cruel branding, because our attitudes are reflected by the producers of children's programmes. The latter know full well who has the ultimate power to distract, divert or even switch off! So what does Bridget's story tell us about ourselves?

Bridget's bus adventure makes me think of boarding a denominational bus. Once we have done that we can assume that we belong, with others, in a unit that is on the move. Whether we like it or not, we all have roles, by the very fact that we have boarded the bus. We may assume that we are type-cast anyway, and behave accordingly; we may have some role thrust upon us by all the others, or we may be given by the Lord a calling that perhaps we had never envisaged.

On the wooden bus the seating was arbitrary. There was no "lead" position; the journey was undertaken two by two. It is as church members have argued about leadership and ministry (servanthood), about the biblical understanding of the words "priest", "bishop" or "deacon", that denominations have sprung into existence to divide the Church. Most of us assume we are "ordinary" and so are not willing to make ourselves available for a role in the denominational bus; however we are very willing to argue the qualities of those we judge fit to take responsibility on our behalf. Some are so closely in tune with Jesus that they are fully aware of their calling, whether it be to preach, prophesy or teach, to heal the sick or encourage others. When we are not in tune with the Lord ourselves these are the ones we are most inclined to reject.

Bridget's bus carried two superficially ineffectual passengers of rank: the policeman and the minister of religion. Both represent government in some way. However we Christians do not seem nearly as much inclined to question the authority of a policeman as we do that of a clergyman.

I grew up in a fairly large village. My father had been brought up in a "low" evangelical Baptist family. Because in my youth the one obvious village church was middle-of-the-way Anglican and he served as parish Treasurer, he seemed to feel it his duty to have regular private altercations with the vicar about the need for biblical precedent in all church activities. However he supported the vicar wholeheartedly amid the public carping which seemed to me to be the inevitable lot of anyone in authority in the Church. This was because the vicar was given the lead so much in the village community that he was made to become virtually a tribal chieftain. He chaired the Public Playing Fields Committee, the Fête Committee, the Committee set up to supervise the Commemorative Public Toilets, and another to protest against the building of those toilets in the first place. All matters connected with the building we called the church were considered to be entirely his responsibility too. If he displeased us in the chairmanship of any of the secular committees or failed to visit anyone known by some to be ill, then he had to accept the fact that help in the church would be withdrawn.

As I grew up I became more and more indignant that a man who tried so hard to please was the butt of everyone's criticism; yet no one could initiate any village activity without first seeking his approval. This was an acceptable situation for the vicar too. However matters became

A Bus-Load of Boffins

distinctly prickly when Christian undertakings had not met with his approval. One day I met him in the village street, looking red-cheeked and flustered.

"I'm sorry, my dear, but I am rather upset. I have just been doing battle with the minister of the Congregational Chapel. He has had the audacity to call upon one of his members who lives in my parish, and to do so without my permission. How dare he? I suppose he knew I'd never give it!"

"But what is wrong with Congregationalists? I believe one or two girls at school are that and they don't seem any different. I know the chapel isn't such an elegant building . . ."

"And they're heretical. Don't you trouble your young head with all that. And when you go up to the university, remember, join the Anglican Society. Watch out for the evangelicals at all costs."

I did. The word intrigued me, because the dictionary said it meant, "of, or according to the teaching of the Gospel of the Christian religion". So I watched out for them and joined them, relieved that I now had no vicar around "to do battle" and stop me.

I was introduced to an even more authoritarian form of ministry when a French family took me to Lourdes to one of the great healing services. Having visited the Grotto where Bernadette received her vision of the Virgin Mary, we joined the crowds surrounding the town square. The sick were laid on stretchers in oval formation. Then some Boy Scouts formed a guard of honour the length of what was to become a processional route. Many groups of pilgrims bearing banners proceeded along this and assembled themselves around specific stretchers. Then the great moment came: all the Scouts knelt as a group of censer-swinging boys and men backed their way before a canopy beneath which ambled a plump prelate. Those backing before him were jostling one another, stepping on each other's toes, set in disarray by the arbitrary swing of the censer. The impatience of the priest beneath the canopy grew from disdain to despair as he tried both to organise his own procession and also to proceed in a way befitting one to whom obeisance was being made. He managed to convey with a gesture peremptory blessings upon the sick, as he passed each stretcher. The surrounding crowds surged in waves to their knees.

"Whoever is this person, that people are kneeling before him, behaving as if he were a god?" I asked my Roman Catholic friend.

"Oh, he's just one of the duty priests," laughed Françoise.

"But why on earth kneel to him and carry a canopy over his head?"

"Because he represents Jesus to us mortals, of course. He is to be revered for that."

I acknowledged that we too call our Anglican clergy "Reverend", one to be revered. I could see how weak and fallible most of them were, because they are "ordinary", like the rest of us. I have since thought about that some more and realise that clergy and ministers of all denominations have taken Holy Orders from Jesus and are to be respected, primarily because they are called to lead His Church. The fact that both Anglicans and Roman Catholics make that abundantly plain by the titles and the roles they undertake is no more alarming than the fact that the Queen expects us to honour and obey those she has appointed to take leadership in her Government.

With the other breath, people talked of the "ministry", of "serving". Jesus was both Lord and servant. How could I begin to sort this out? Jesus allowed Thomas to call Him "My Lord and my God!" (John 20:28) and Peter to declare, "Thou art the Christ, the Son of the living God" (Matt. 16:16 AV). We do the same, knowing that Jesus is our only Lord. But Jesus, our Lord and Master, is also our servant and tells us categorically that we are to wash one another's feet, to be servants of one another (John 13:14). Nowhere does Jesus allocate roles and titles of respect to us; we who were at one time specifically His servants have become specifically His friends (John 15:15). Friends have the honour of each other's confidence; they know what each other is up to, and have no need to attribute titles, because the mutual reverence is there anyway.

When we lived in Washington, DC I became friendly with a dentist's widow. Phyllis was called to the ministry of the Episcopalian Church and so, having been authorised by her bishop, she went to the State Seminary for training. By the time she graduated she had *cum laude* qualifications in both preaching and pastoral care. In fact she graduated first in her year in the latter. There was one big snag: the Episcopalian Church did not then recognise women as priests. Phyllis was well aware of this and it did not strike either of us that she should begin a militant campaign to establish her rights. All Phyllis knew was that she had been called to the ministry and that that call had been ratified and confirmed, first by the bishop and afterwards by academic and spiritual examination. Slightly puzzled that, unlike her fellows, she had been offered no easy initial placement, she handed the whole matter over in prayer to God and got on with the business of living.

One day the telephone in my kitchen rang.

"Hi, doll! What d'you make of this?" the relaxed voice drawled. "An ad in the *Post*. Got today's edition? Look in the Employment Section." We had no regular copy of this gigantic publication. "Well, looks like I'm to read it out to you, gal. Listening?

"WANTED! (Great to be wanted, isn't it?) Men willing to work: outside, town and city; inside, office or home; with the poor; with professionals; with the bone idle; with workaholics! Low pay. All the hours there are! CAN

THIS BE YOU?
For more details, write or call: The United Church of Christ."

"Sounds all right to me, if you're that sort," I conceded. "Never heard of them, myself. Are they OK?"

"C'm on, kid. Same as English United Reformed Church, to all intents and purposes. Dunno whether they mean Men or men, though. S'pose that could be a limiting factor."

Phyllis wrote a letter of hope — "You sound the right people for the ministry I'm called to" — laced with speculation — "Do you mean 'men' generically, or 'men' as opposed to women?" The United Reformed Church meant the first and so Phyllis was interviewed and accepted without hesitation for ordination.

Once the formalities were over, her one wry comment was, "Funny thing is, kid, I had all my Episcopalian clergy tutors lay hands on me during the ceremony. So am I or am I not part of the Apostolic Succession?!"

Whatever the apostles were originally appointed to, Phyllis was destined to almost unremitting servanthood, beginning with numerous summer burials while her colleagues were on vacation. I heard from her long after our return to England. Always she was on her own, carrying out the work of a servant, but with the lonely authority attributed to her by those she pastored. She was paid and housed by the congregation as long as she preached and did what pleased them.

While Phyllis was struggling to fulfil her Lord's call to ministry, in her case such solitary responsibility, Hugh and I had discovered the Potter's House, a restaurant in downtown Washington. The food, the atmosphere, the live music, the hand-made crockery and the service were excellent. This did not surprise us once we read the small print on the back of the menu: "All who serve in this coffee shop are ministers in the Church of the Saviour." I looked around me. Those preparing or bringing food to tables, those deep in conversation with customers and those clearing dishes or washing up, each was individual in clothes, manner, culture and even colour. The one quality common to all was that they were serving, gladly and lovingly. Hugh and I soon discovered the church of which the Potter's House ministry was only a part. We were told that everyone who satisfactorily completed a two-year membership course became a minister. So far there were seventy.

"Who's my minister, then?" I asked my course instructor, a sixty-year-old widow.

"I am, I think," smiled Martha. "I think I'm the member who lives nearest to you. One moment. How many miles is it from Wisconsin Circle to here? Perhaps Dupont Circle is nearer."

"What I mean is, who would help me if there was a crisis?"

"Depends what sort. We all would, of course, according to our gifts and qualifications. If someone's ill, David's a doctor. Or perhaps you need family advice — now let me think who's good on marriage counselling."

"I really meant, who'd come if there was something really important, like a birth or death?"

"Oh, I would, because I'm nearest. And you could tell Elizabeth Ann. Her daughter's marvellous with babies."

"Wouldn't Gordon Cosby come?"

"Gordon? Well, he's the founder and he does represent us when the leaders of the various Washington churches get together. But whyever should you need his attentions particularly? He does live way out in Mount Vernon."

I had no answer. I had always assumed that someone somewhere was human boss of whatever church I attended. Each member of that church should, in my estimation, be subject to that boss's decisions, inasmuch as that member chose to become involved in what the church provided for spiritual sustenance, entertainment or worship. I looked again at the membership commitment that could one day make me one of the many ministers of that church:

> I come today to join the local expression of the Church, which is the body of those on whom the call of God rests to witness to the grace and truth of God.
>
> I recognise that the function of the Church is to glorify God in adoration and sacrificial service, and to be God's missionary to the world, bearing witness to God's redeeming grace in Jesus Christ.
>
> I believe as did Peter that Jesus is the Christ, the Son of the Living God.
>
> I unreservedly and with abandon commit my life and destiny to Christ, promising to give Him a practical priority in all the affairs of life. I will seek first the Kingdom of God and His Righteousness.
>
> I commit myself, regardless of the expenditures of time, energy and money, to becoming an informed, mature Christian.
>
> I believe that God is the total owner of my life and resources. I give God the throne in relation to the material aspect of my life. God is the owner. I am the ower. Because God is a lavish giver I too shall be lavish and cheerful in my regular gifts.
>
> I will seek to be Christian in all relations with my fellowman, with other nations, groups, classes and races.
>
> I will seek to bring every phase of my life under the Lordship of Christ.
>
> When I move from this place I will join some other expression of the Christian Church.

This commitment was something way beyond the "take-it-

or-leave-it'' involvement or detachment to which I had grown accustomed in adult life.

The words "unreservedly and with abandon" worried me a little. I was used to retaining my right to reservations, to modifying my judgment as I learned more. Disciplined thinking was never carried out "with abandon". I thought again about Phyllis. Her mind was essentially disciplined, her behaviour reserved. Then one day I had heard from her son that she had died in early middle age. Alone, I suspect, and partly, I suspect, of disillusionment. Once and once only, unreservedly and with abandon, as we left the United States she had given us something childlike: a burgundy, velvet-robed archangel to crown our Christmas tree every year "in memory", as she put it then, "of me". This beautiful, lavishly dressed, semi-human archangel was not characteristic of the scholar I had known. Yet somehow it expressed her deep desire to be accepted in the midst of family festivities in an uncomplicated household where children mattered. Phyllis's archangel now ministers in great joy in our midst at Christmas, at the top of the tree!

Phyllis worked mostly alone. But the Church of the Saviour ministers were there to care for one another, as well as for the congregation. Twenty years later when I returned I found the same spirit of covenant still strong. It seems that they were acting upon what they knew so well, that every member of Christ's body has a function and that every function is essential to the well-being of the whole:

For the body does not consist of one member but of many. If the foot should say, "Because I am not a hand, I do not belong to the body," that would not make it any less a part of the body. And if the ear should say, "Because I am not an eye I do not belong to the body," that would not make it any less a part of the body. If the whole body were an eye, where would be the hearing? . . . But as it is, God arranged the organs in the body, each one as he chose. (1 Cor. 12:14–18)

What structures, then, are necessary? We can learn from all the denominations. There is room for careful and God-directed pastoring of the flock. The charismatics are usually insistent about that; but there is plenty to learn from the parish structures of the Church of England. Even if my village vicar sometimes became exclusive in his denominationalism, he really did watch over his flock, whether or not they came to church. The Roman Catholic priest at Lourdes was there to remind us all that someone was around who knew both how to respect Christ and how to try to be His representative in concern for the sick. It is moving to see how Phyllis's valiant attempts, first in the Episcopalian Church and then in the United Church of Christ, to obey her call to serve and minister led her into a corner where there was no one to serve and minister to her.

As a renewed Christian observing those who were dissatisfied with the main-line denominations they had left, I came out of Anglicanism briefly and took my children to the Methodist Church, where I knew there was a thriving Bible-based Sunday School and where I knew that the structures allowed some of the renewed Christians in the congregation to undertake the ministries to which they were called. What challenged me most of all was the Methodist Covenant service:

> I am no longer my own, but Thine. Put me to what Thou wilt; put me to doing, put me to suffering; let me be employed for Thee or laid aside for Thee, exalted for Thee or brought low for Thee; let me be full, let me be empty; let me have all things, let me have nothing; I freely and heartily yield all things to Thy pleasure and disposal. And now, O glorious and blessed God, Father, Son and Holy Spirit, Thou art mine and I am Thine. So be it. And the

Covenant which I have made on earth, let it be ratified in heaven. Amen.

Then I realised that I could not merely follow my own preferences. My role in the Body of Christ was to be at His disposal. That involved a willingness not to be used, and that was potentially hard. Gradually I sensed that abandoning the Anglicans, however temporarily, added to the hurt and brokenness of the Body of Christ. Eventually Hugh and I had to acknowledge there was much that was good in both denominations and both ministries, and we took joint membership of both churches.

We were particularly content with the liturgy of the Anglican Alternative Service Book, because however feeble and lacking our own worship and prayer we were in tune with the words used. The Methodist service, on the other hand, seemed to depend for its content on the personal choice of the preacher for the day. When it came to ministry the Methodists were only too happy with members caring for members in town or village, whereas there was very little I could do in an Anglican parish without the full authorisation of the vicar. This became clear when some of those the Good News van had visited with library books asked me to return and discuss personal problems with borrowers, who were growing fast as they read. Each borrower was in a geographical parish, whatever his denomination. It was essential that the Good News team linked with the vicar, informing him of difficulties, telling him what we were doing. However in many parishes in our van area there was an interregnum. Services were arranged by the Rural Dean but he had little personal knowledge of the parishioners in the district, many of whom were not connected with the Anglican Church and had invited us to come as personal friends.

Nevertheless, in order to reassure the doubtful, it is sometimes necessary to show a piece of paper authorising pastoral ministry. Rural Evangelism (Mission for Christ) organisation makes sure that everyone connected with it has a "visiting card" designating him as "worker", or in my case "fully accredited member". I have a friend Mary who was quite unnerved by the clergy. They were well aware of the discourtesy of poaching in someone else's parish and convinced Mary that that rule ought to apply to lay ministry too. Mary wrote to her bishop telling him how, when she was about seventeen, she had had a call from the Lord to "teach and tend his lambs". In her daily life as a teacher and house-group leader there was plenty of opportunity to do this. However, as she had often visited the bishop for personal consultation, she felt it might be helpful if he could send her some sort of authorisation for the informal pastoral work she was being invited to do in the parishes of his diocese.

He replied that he was writing to the suffragan bishop, asking him to meet Mary. Would she please telephone him and arrange this? She tells me she felt weary and hesitant as she drove through the darkness of a winter evening to discover what the bishop could supply by way of a useful little document for her to present to the dubious. The bishop was warmly encouraging and at the end of a really interesting evening, came to the point.

"Well, now, about this ordination business. I suggest that's your best way forward."

"Ordination?" she questioned inside herself. "I wasn't thinking of that, Lord; only a bit of paper . . ."

"So I'll write to the Diocesan Director of Ordinands. He'll interview you and we'll go on from there."

"But, Lord, I didn't really want to do that," she protested. "That's not my scene, being out in front, taking services."

"Thank you very much," she said aloud. Then, with real enthusiasm, "Thank you for a lovely evening, the talk about poetry and for the coffee."

Mary drove home bemused. "Lord, I don't know quite what this is all about. But if that's what you want, I'll go ahead. I suppose only time will tell why I'm having to go through all this." She added as an afterthought, "I'm not telling Henry yet, Lord. Perhaps you don't really mean it. Then I'd feel so stupid, especially after all I've already said to my husband about Anglican clergy having to carry the can for everything."

Some weeks later she was in the office of the DDO. She looked around at the books on his shelves. They were the sort that she used to find in the basement of Mowbray's in Cambridge, the sort she thought all theologians ought to read some day, the sort she would not dream of putting on the church bookstall for which she was the buyer. Few ordinary church visitors would think of casually picking them up and even fewer would find them absorbing reading. She realised that her interviewer probably led a rigorous academic life by the very nature of his office as Director of Ordinands. His friendly questions soon bore this out.

"Would you be prepared to travel either to Lincoln or to Nottingham one evening each week for three years?"

Inside herself she remonstrated with the Lord. "It's forty miles to Lincoln, thirty-five or forty to Nottingham. Every week? What will happen to the four children, Lord? Henry's far too busy to spend much time with them. At the end of a day's teaching, Lord? I can't abandon my house-groups. Are you sure I'm up to it? You have confirmed my calling to the work I'm already doing, again and again, but this is really puzzling."

"All you have to do at the moment is listen," came the quiet voice in her mind.

"What about your family? We'd like them all to come in the summer to a house-party, so that we can meet them." Mary pictured her four teenage children. They had attended both Spring Harvest and Greenbelt Festival and were now intelligently working out their own Christian way. "Anyway, for the time being, I'd like you to meet a woman deacon. She's a clergy wife." He handed Mary a telephone number. "Make an appointment with her, will you?"

The interview that followed was much more gruelling. The deacon's life seemed to be really interesting, because she was chaplain at a Further Education College, similar to the one where Mary had taught history. Mary had thoroughly enjoyed the people she met in that work and was fascinated to see how stringent the chaplain's questions were. She had not been prepared for this kind of searching interview and came away a little relieved at the realisation that she would probably now be turned down for training.

However very soon afterwards there was a visit to her home by the DDO. Poor Henry, who had had the matter only vaguely explained to him, was nonplussed at the rate matters were moving. However he was always interested in anything to do with the Anglican clergy and especially in women's ordination, and was his usual loyal and supportive self, "if this is really what my wife had intended. I just wonder whatever the point of it is."

The next step was to explain the situation to Mary's vicar. He had never shown any particular interest in her work and was suspicious of the interdenominational house-group she ran. But Henry and Mary had been members of his church for thirteen years.

"You know there will be no room for you to preach in my pulpit. I already have a curate, a lay-reader and a deacon, and the town is swarming with retired clergy."

"That's the last thing I had in mind. I've no thoughts of an out-front ministry."

"And I'll have no charismatic goings-on."

"Whatever do you mean?" She was puzzled that anyone as mild as herself in worship should be suspected of "charismatic goings-on".

"Banging tambourines, waving your arms about, clapping . . ."

A Bus-Load of Boffins

Mary described to me afterwards the looks of total astonishment exchanged by the choir when friendly visitors standing with her in the front row of the congregation had had the temerity to raise an arm in proclamation as the whole congregation sang "Thine be the glory!" She had been so embarrassed that, disloyally, she had not joined them; however the hearts of several further back in the congregation had been much uplifted.

"But I wouldn't have a chance if I had no out-front ministry," she affirmed. "What I am really called to do is pastoral work, as I've told you."

"I'd give you a short list of specific names. You would visit them and them alone."

Silently she questioned the Lord. "Are you trying to discipline me? How would I explain this to the people who have already asked me to come? They expect me regularly. I'd be letting down real friends."

"Your job is only to listen, still," came the silent answer. "What you need to do is to get to know the congregation."

Mary was silent for a little. Having lived and worshipped in the town for over a decade she knew all but the latest newcomers.

"Yes, I'd like to get to know the new ones. How about a church house-group or two?"

"House-groups are not popular in this parish. They are really only holy huddles. We meet together at the Parish Communion. The rest of the week should be spent out in the world. No, if you are to get to know the church, come on one of our coach outings. We're off to Skegness one Saturday soon."

Again Mary thought of her husband and children. Saturday was the day they did all the things they enjoyed or had to catch up with. A parish coach outing would be howled down.

"Well, that's that, then. Get to know the parish and off you go for your training."

She was ushered to the door, bewildered.

"Now I want you to assess the situation. I have called you to teach and tend my sheep. Can you do it best by entering the full-time Anglican ministry in this town? Do you have no opportunity to do what I've asked you to do as things stand?"

"Of course I have every opportunity, Lord. But that doesn't go down very well among those who will only relate to someone with authority."

"Are those the people I'm sending you to?"

Of course, the answer was no. When Mary got home and explained her dilemma, someone remarked, "But people know you as a sound and trustworthy teacher and friend. Just go in the name of Jesus and trust Him for the outcome."

So she telephoned the DDO's answering machine and put the whole matter on ice.

After that Henry and Mary found they were given pastoral work as ordinary members of the congregation. A clear list allocated to them in the area of their general ministry proved to be interesting, friendly people whom they could get to know really well.

Henry's question, "Whatever is the point of your being ordained?" was at the heart of everything to do with their work with the Lord. All Mary was really being asked to do was to respond to people's invitations to come to them, to get on with the job. We do not necessarily have to be in any position of authority. The confirmation of the rightness lies in the need being fulfilled as we obey. Bridget's bus passengers went looking for authority figures in time of crisis. When Milly fell down it did not occur to Rose that she was the closest "minister" to hand. In time of need, each one on board was a boffin.

The tapestry stool which I had sewn depicted other toys as well as the bus passengers. As Milly lay in need of rescue, a knitted chinless Piglet swung from the J of Jane

A Bus-Load of Boffins

(Penelope's middle name), observing and reporting the scene, commentating on the way in which this bus-load of boffins was managing. Similarly the world watches all of us attempting to be the Church and making a similar mess of it.

Renewed, or charismatic, Christians have so withdrawn from the mistakes of the established denominations that the world can observe us, living in a dried-out "Noddy" land, where we fear anything but bright, simple, childlike symbols, songs and ways of worship.

In the end we have to become again like little children, but this time with the humility to be able to discern what is still honourable, just, pure, excellent, wise and true in the old denominations. If we reach back in them in love, our desire to become united as a community can be refined and disciplined, our yearning to commune with our Heavenly Father can be informed and enriched, and our service and ministry one to another can be welded into the whole that Jesus so longed for in His prayer before His crucifixion: "that they may be one, even as we are one" (John 17:11). In the bus story it was big Bridget who eventually came to the rescue of that bus-load of tiny boffins, set them to rights and blessed them. For us it is our Heavenly Father who does that.

The mechanical role of the fat little priest has a profound significance for us all. Denis Ball, in *Praying in the Spirit* points out how important a blessing is. He says, "it is the pronouncing or invoking, through a mental and spiritual giving that which is in agreement with God's will to benefit the recipient (or situation) with happiness, healing or some other remedy". The person conferring the blessing must first be in a right relationship with God, in order for him to be a channel of untarnished goodness. He must have received from Jesus whatever cleansing he needs. He must also will goodness and fulfilment towards the one who is to receive the blessing. That involves a concerned awareness of the other person's needs. Then we have to be open for the Holy Spirit to use us, if He wishes, as glad channels of His love, joy and fulfilment. Even a little child can do that.

Each of us is free to be used in the ministry of blessing. The retired ninety-year-old Mother Abbess of Malling Abbey used blessing as a farewell: "Christ in you! Christ in all! Christ, all in all!"

What abundance of life and what reverence for all mankind there then is in those simple words, "Blessings on you, my child!"

10

"ALL GONE, A DEVIL!"

The room smelt of baby talc and damp hair. Amid chortles of laughter I had chased Penelope as she rampaged stark naked across the landing, determined to have a romp before being tucked up in bed. Now, firmly fastened into her sleeping suit she was climbing on to my lap, armed with her favourite books, *The Very Hungry Caterpillar*, and the Piccolo Children's Bible opened as always at the picture of Jesus fastidiously shoving away a bright green, fat, most unattractive devil. As I read the story of the Temptations, Penelope turned the page for me as soon as possible with a triumphant, "All gone, a devil. All gone! OH, dear!"

The next page was almost as much fun, because the same picture of a very ordinary-looking Jesus was now awash with golden angels — and they looked almost as beautiful as the ones in the earlier pictures of the newborn baby Jesus. Penelope would then embark upon her "Thank-you-Gods", which involved thanking Jesus for everything, from playing peep-bo under the sweater worn by her home-made friend Pooh Bear, to helping push the pram containing her very new sister "Chooliet".

In some ways we are like children when we first become members of the Church. Full of expectation, we are ready to love every aspect of it. We try to join in, just as small Juliet had at Parish Communion, and we try to understand why things are as they are, as Rupert had challenged us by putting the tea-bag out to be aired, demanding of us all why it was necessary to live so frugally as to allow life to lose its flavour.

When the young man Jesus first began His ministry, He too was thrilled to be able to tell the congregation at His home town, Nazareth, that Isaiah's prophecy about bringing liberty and healing was that day beginning to be fulfilled.

Penelope was not permitted to develop far enough to challenge much. Within seven weeks of Juliet's birth she was to develop a great "head hurts" one day, lapse into a coma the next and on the third day, die. Suddenly it was time for both her and us to grow up.

She had loved a lively romp, revelled in the fun of her family, was thrilled at the miracle of her baby sister's tiny hands and feet, and especially liked seeing that bright green lump of a devil disappear on the next page of her Children's Bible. Death, in the form of a cancerous brain tumour, had not revealed its presence until three days before the end. Penelope was only two and three-quarters. She had no opportunity to enquire the purpose of the agony of that final headache. Presumably now she knows and can understand. However it was time for me to be willing to be made to grow up into a fuller understanding of God's ways.

The windows of Coventry Cathedral gave me some guidance. They are recessed, so that one cannot see them until one has passed them. They represent stages of our lives, culminating in old age and entry into eternity. The final south window, the one on the end of the right-hand wall nearest the tapestry of Christ in glory, is made up of myriad fragments of glass, all translucent except one tiny piece at adult eye-level. This is a dirty shard of mirror. Coming across that, I am reminded of Paul's words in 1 Corinthians 13:11–12:

When I was a child, I spoke like a child, I thought like a child, I reasoned like a child; when I became a man,

I gave up childish ways. For now we see in a mirror dimly, but then face to face. Now I know in part; then I shall understand fully, even as I have been fully understood.

On this side of eternity, Paul says, we can understand ourselves and events only murkily; in fact the light of Truth is blocked by a grubby mirror, reflecting only our meagre earthly selves.

Once we have passed along the aisle of thorns in Coventry Cathedral we arrive at the tapestry of Christ seated in glory; alongside Him and from His vantage point, we can perceive the whole pattern of the recessed windows which signify our lives. They make a logical and beautiful sequence. Although our journey to be with Jesus must entail the suffering signified by thorns, even those contribute to the ordered formation of the whole.

I have told in a chapter in *Facing Bereavement*, edited by Ann Warren, how I came to understand as Penelope lay dying that it would be best for my daughter, best for me, best somehow for everyone, if I could only allow the Lord to take sole charge of this situation, let Him have His way. In doing this I somehow joined both Jesus and Penelope in shoving off that green, eternally ridiculous devil. Death now become the joyful gateway into glory, was itself defeated; the devil's purposes were thwarted.

Soon there was every indication that Penelope's life was continuing, sinfree at last and full. Not only that, but I became aware also that through the different personal ministries of believers all around me the resurrected Body of Christ, His Church, was beginning to be clearly discernible. A neighbour did all the cooking for the post-funeral party on Penelope's birthday into heaven. An uncle brought a big box of onions, "to help you cry". Friends from the Church in Washington where Penelope had worshipped with us, wrote giving us great spiritual boosts to go on in the name of the Lord, praising Him for Penelope.

Above all I noticed how friends and relations were at last being reconciled. When I was growing up family feuds had hatched and been fed, so that I knew who was not speaking to whom, mostly because of financial disagreements over wills. The comment common to all these arguments was, "I want absolutely nothing to do with X. It's all so very petty!" But Penelope was the proud possessor of a mere two shillings and sixpence, given to her by a cleaning lady at her Daddy's school; so the conversation was different. I heard them this time trying to comfort and explain to one another the death of a loving little girl. In the face of Death, as in the face of the Second World War, the relatives were uniting again. Truth and Love must at last be permitted to prevail in the face of this common enemy.

Penelope had enjoyed seeing the disappearance of the fat green devil in her Bible, but of course she had had no opportunity to take real interest in the grown-up Jerusalem Bible given to her by one of her godmothers, an ecumenically-minded German Roman Catholic. On the flyleaf Hildegard had written:

There is one Lord, one faith, one baptism, and one God who is Father of all, over all, through all and within all. (Eph. 4:5–6 JB)

At Penelope's funeral she added:

He made her clean by washing her in water with a form of words, so that when he took her to himself she would be glorious, with no spot or wrinkle or anything like that, but holy and faultless. (Eph. 5:26–27)

Hildegard narrowed down what initially had described the redeemed Church, the spotless Bride of Christ, to apply momentarily at least to one little girl. Mostly Penelope's relationship with Jesus consisted in loving both Him and

"All Gone, a Devil!"

without exception everyone around her; and in thanking Jesus for the whole of each day.

As we all know only too well, the Bride of Christ is by no means yet spotless. In terms of unity we all see only ourselves mirrored in that murky shard of glass. We are broken, tainted with malice and pride. The Church is constantly suffering from communal and individual sin; the Body of Christ has been torn apart and scarred by warring denominations. Despite annual Weeks of Prayer for Unity, the world may well comment with sarcasm, "See how these Christians set themselves apart from one another." However once I became renewed in the Holy Spirit I began to see, at first in poor focus as a toddler, but eventually with increasingly clear vision, how all the facets of Christian belief were not contradictory but rather contributory to the whole truth. No longer was there much point in belonging exclusively to one particular denomination. All Christians have access to the truth once they have Jesus, who *is* that Truth, as Lord. As the Holy Spirit highlights parts of Scripture for us we become fascinated as more and more of the Bible becomes intelligible and significant in daily life. It is no longer a hardship or embarrassment for us to share with one another what we are discovering: "I will put my laws into their minds, and write them on their hearts, and I will be their God and they shall be my people. And they shall not teach everyone his fellow . . . for all shall know me, from the least of them to the greatest" (Heb. 8:10–11).

After all we constantly face a common enemy, Satan. We are in a spiritual world war all the time. This does not become evident unless or until we are willing to step out in faith and proclaim Jesus as King. Then the attacks come! But then too God's family can see beyond petty rifts of denominational bias among "the relations". Once the enemy has been sighted, then those who are committed to the Lord will muster, sharing all, so that each part of the Body can be equipped for battle royal! As soon as He had announced the tremendous news in Nazareth, that Isaiah's prophecy of liberation was that day beginning to be fulfilled in Himself, Jesus was made thoroughly aware of the enmity latent in those around Him. Despite the fact that initially they all spoke well of Him, He knew that "no prophet is acceptable in his own country" (Luke 4:24). Very soon He was trying to teach His disciples about His own passion. The suffering and rejection in the face of evil was inevitable.

When I was trying to sort out in my own mind how to answer those who challenged me about God's very existence as well as about His seemingly heartless personality, I found reassurance not only in the Bible, for instance in the Book of Job, but also in the lively Christian paperbacks which soon became real friends. I have told in *Out of the Ark* how deeply they affected my life: for example in *The Hiding Place*, Corrie ten Boom's new-found ability to forgive the ultimate hurts of the cruel deaths of both her father and sister; Catherine Marshall's *Something More*, in which a new power received from God enabled her similarly to forgive others and to allow the Holy Spirit to empower her life; Urquhart's *When the Spirit Comes*; and Dennis Bennett's *Nine o'Clock in the Morning*. These books were to transform my own life.

When I saw with new eyes why people around me were suffering from the centuries-old malaise which was causing so many terrible divisions in the Church, I longed that they too should be renewed and fed by such books, so that together we could know the hope, love and joy of real unity. Christians in and around Stamford began to share this longing to shove off for ever the Devil of Disunity. The Holy Spirit inspired many from each of the denominations to pray and thereafter to take action, so that the Ark Christian Book and Coffee Shop came into being.

However there was a dimension beyond this that the Lord wanted to use. He gives us anything we ask, provided it is in accordance with His fatherly care of us, and now He

"All Gone, a Devil!"

wanted to answer the prayers of those who needed to feed on Christian books without buying them. People who were groping after God and others who claimed Jesus as Lord could unite, regardless of denomination or lack of it, in borrowing books freely from the library vans dotted all over Britain. These little Good News vans, manned by a team of two, were willing to come wherever invited, loaded with contemporary Christian paperbacks. As they returned month by month bringing different and new supplies, friendships were established and churches fortified. The rifts in God's Church were being healed as book- and tape-borrowers became renewed in the power of the Holy Spirit, equipped to bear the fruits of love and hope among their neighbours. At the time of writing there are twenty-seven of these small library vans, fully taxed, stocked and insured, provided by God's people as they are inspired to give.

It seems to me that our Lord is determined to make full use of the suffering and division caused by Evil. The death of my daughter brought me into a new relationship not only with my Heavenly Father but also with other people. I began to grow up in my Christian life. Just as Jesus' awareness of the evil around Him showed Him that the way to glory was to be through His passion and crucifixion, so the Church too must mature in love, on through the agonies of division until Jesus brings it relief and unity at last by freeing it of sin. In some small way Jesus is using the library vans to achieve His purpose of unity, by drawing people together in the ordinariness of a home and feeding them.

Recently I have discovered that God is doing a new thing. It took me a long time to see it!

Before the Down family came to share the work of the Good News Trust I had been involved in house-groups which could not depend on the wisdom of a highly-qualified theologian, mostly because they happened to have come together as a result of a Good News van visit. People had a new hunger to understand the Bible better. So we would select a passage, usually from the Good News Bible because this was easy to read and understand. It was very much like sitting around a casserole informally at a supper party.

One would say, "This looks delicious!" ("I've always wanted to study John's Gospel and I'm looking forward to doing so.")

"Yes, it certainly smells good." ("The inklings I have of it, for instance when I've heard it read in church, are very attractive — so far.")

Another, warily moving something to the side of her plate: "I'm not sure about these little black bits. Did something get burnt?" ("I don't like this bit that says you can't even *see* the Kingdom unless you're born again.")

"But these are mushrooms and they're delicious!" ("But the joy of it is, you *are* born again — and so can anybody else be if they're willing — and so you have the tremendous privilege of being able to see something of what Jesus is doing in the world today.")

In this way the "nasty little black bits" of the Bible became the tastiest part of the whole casserole, the transforming seasoning, perhaps, the joy of the wonderful new life of the Kingdom where Jesus is really supreme.

Martin Down was a theologian by training, I a graduate teacher. Together we looked again at the foundation passage for the Good News Trust, the Feeding of the Five Thousand (Luke 9:11–17). If we asked the Lord to guide us, we too could "sit them down in companies and feed them ourselves" with whatever the Lord taught us from His word. Mary told the disciples, "Do whatever he tells you" (John 2:5). We knew that all we had to do was concoct questions which the Holy Spirit would take and use so that as people discussed possible answers they would begin to realise what the Lord required of them. Each would be enlightening the others, provided we all prayed about the food the Lord was giving. The practical Bible Study material, the "Do-Its", soon became available and were disseminated free of charge

"All Gone, a Devil!"

to any house-group, preferably interdenominational, that asked for them.

One day I received an order for a hundred sets of a course entitled Neighbourly Evangelism. "Oh, dear!" I grumbled to myself. "A vicar's ordered this just because it sounds a good pew-filler." When we were compiling these studies Martin and I had agreed between ourselves that anyone undertaking evangelism ought to be empowered first by the Holy Spirit. In order to ensure this we recommended that, if appropriate, it would be good to study what we called a Foundation Course first. Once I had summoned enough courage, after several cups of coffee and the excuses of lunch preparation and washing up, I telephoned the vicar of Lowerstone, as I shall call it. To my relief and delight his wife answered.

"Of course we're all renewed in the Holy Spirit. Don't you remember sending us your Baptism in the Holy Spirit course?"

Had she not sounded so reassuring, with every evidence that she knew what I was talking about, I would have felt a complete fool. As it was, I had a new friend at the other end of the telephone miles away in Hampshire. I packed up the parcel and gladly put the bright orange order form to join others on a bull-dog clip, where they hung from a nail and accumulated for no particular purpose — or so I thought.

Some months afterwards I received a call from a friend I shall call Brenda. We had met at the holiday venue in Anglesey, but Brenda's home was a cottage near Warwick. Now matters were worrying her uncharacteristically.

"Frightfully sorry to phone you out of nowhere, as it were. No, it's not about Anglesey, though I wish it was! Well, it's perfectly stupid of me, but I want you to, er, think of me next Tuesday. I'll be in hospital. Well, it's nothing really, just a bit of bowel trouble, cancer, actually, nothing to worry about. Just pray, please, because I feel stupidly frightened and I'll be miles from home. Why? Well, that's a long story; Lowerstone District Hospital, somewhere in Hampshire. Just get praying. Bye-eee!"

"Whatever can I do to help Brenda, Lord? Please help her because I just can't. Warwick's miles away. It would take half a day to go and pray with her — and anyway she wouldn't want it!" I had wandered upstairs to the loo for a private think. "And of course Hampshire's out of the question. Whatever would the family do while I'm buzzing off across London to someone who'll be unconscious and in the operating theatre before I get there?"

Into my mind's eye came a picture of the batch of vibrant orange order forms hanging from a nail in the study.

"That's nothing to do with today and now. I'm worried for Brenda. What can I do, Lord?"

Then I realised. Lowerstone: Baptism in the Holy Spirit. "We know what you're talking about . . ." I was off immediately, telephoning, this time with confidence and purpose.

"Yes, Good News Trust here. I've got a job for you or one of your parishioners. Please will you visit the District Hospital on Tuesday and pray for Mrs Brenda Oldham. She's being admitted for a cancer operation."

"Do whatever He tells you."

Brenda phoned me on the Wednesday evening to say that the vicar had visited her within an hour of her arrival, that whatever happened in the future something very wonderful had happened for her, that she was quite sure all would be well, in the very best sense of all, because one of the Family had visited and prayed with her.

That apparently insignificant wad of orange order forms had meaning at last. In the Lowerstone incident was incontrovertible evidence that God was using His people, in a living network of renewed Christians of all denominations right across Britain. As I looked at the hundreds of green specks located on the map of Britain

"All Gone, a Devil!"

where these house-groups were, I realised that in most cases they were gathered near a tiny red dot, signifying the unassuming presence of a solitary van team, and that van team would not have come into existence had I not been made to look at life afresh, because of Penelope's death, to see God at work and to join in as He directed. All other renewed Christians of every denomination had something to contribute to the whole, because each had some unique understanding or way of worship that could enlighten life in the Holy Spirit.

Gradually we are all emerging from the childhood of spiritual experience, so that we can be welded together beyond the point where others merely note how we love one another. Eventually Jesus will build us up to become His perfect Body, made up of innumerable denominations, roles and parts, but all eventually attaining to "the unity of the faith . . . to mature manhood, to the measure of the stature of the fullness of Christ . . . from whom the whole body, joined and knit together . . . upbuilds itself in love" (Eph. 4:13–16).

But in the end we can begin to do this only, as Eliot puts it in his *Four Quartets*, "in a condition of complete simplicity, costing not less than everything".

REFERENCES

Allan, Rosalind, *Out of the Ark*. Hodder, 1986.
Ball, Denis, *Praying in the Spirit*. Darton Longman & Todd, 1989.
Bennett, Dennis, *Nine o'Clock in the Morning*. Coverdale House, 1974.
Eliot, T.S., *Four Quartets*. Faber, 1979.
Lewis, C.S., *Out of the Silent Planet*. Pan Books, 1968.
Marshall, Catherine, *Something More*. Hodder, 1977.
Schlink, Basilea, *Realities*. Lakeland, 1967.
ten Boom, Corrie, *The Hiding Place*. Hodder, 1976.
Urquhart, Colin, *When the Spirit Comes*. Hodder, 1974.
Warren, Ann, ed., *Facing Bereavement*. Highland, 1988.

Also available in Hodder Christian Paperback

WHAT IS THE NEW AGE?

Michael Cole, Jim Graham, Tony Higton, David Lewis

Channelling, ley lines, veganism, reincarnation, environmental concern, belief in astral bodies, telepathy, healing, spiritualism: these have all been associated with the New Age.

But what exactly is the New Age? Is it simply ancient Eastern religion dressed up in new Western clothes? Is it compatible with the Christian faith? Is it a worldwide conspiracy to usher in the one-world government of the Anti-Christ?

The authors set out to give authoritative answers to questions such as these, and to discover the origins of the thought behind this fast-growing system of beliefs.

THE GUINNESS LEGEND

Michele Guinness

When the first Arthur Guinness founded a small brewery on the banks of the River Liffey in Dublin, he could not have foreseen the dynasty of brewers and bankers that would emerge. But there was another side to the family: several generations of brilliant clergymen and missionaries, perhaps the greatest being Henry Grattan Guinness, the Billy Graham of his day.

Drawing on letters and diaries, Michele Guinness tells of the adventures of Henry Grattan Guinness and his spirited and talented children, interweaving the adventures with the successes and failures of their brewing and banking counterparts.

'A fascinating story'

The Scotsman

'A thorough, informative but above all captivating account of a truly outstanding family.'

Sunday Tribune, Dublin

'There is adventure and colour here and an admirable vitality; one comes to be fond of them, for they were talented, amusing and brave.' Jonathan Guinness.

Literary Review

THE STORM AND OTHER STORIES

Jenny Cooke

Cari, weighed down by the burden of poverty, a drunken father and an unwelcome suitor, has a prophetic dream about a storm which hits the village of Anglesey. When it actually happens, it brings unexpected blessing. *The Storm* opens this collection of short stories. All based on fact and set against richly varied historical backgrounds, these stories speak of transforming faith and the tenacity of hope in the face of pain, disappointment and hardship. Some have been broadcast on Radio Manchester.

Jenny Cooke is the popular author of *Cross Behind Bars* and *Upon this Rock*. She is also a columnist for Renewal magazine.